A Message from Jakie

A Message from Jakie

A Spiritual Journey of Love, Death, and Hope

Michael Weinberger

SENTIENT PUBLICATIONS

Cover design by Kim Johansen
Book design by Nicholas Cummings

Library of Congress Cataloging-in-Publication Data

Weinberger, Michael.
  A message from Jakie / by Michael Weinberger. -- 1st Sentient
Publications ed.
    p. cm.
  ISBN 1-59181-043-4
  1. Weinberger, Michael. 2. Weinberger, Jakie (Spirit) 3. Spiritual
biography--United States.   I. Title.
BL73.W42A3 2006
133.9092--dc22
[B]

                                                2005037617

SENTIENT PUBLICATIONS, LLC
1113 Spruce Street
Boulder, CO 80302
www.sentientpublications.com

Contents

A MESSAGE FROM JAKE

Love me as a light spirit
- as an angel - as a
radiant ember of living light.

See me as even more vibrant and alive now!
I am free and exploding, expanding, expanding,
expanding, expanding. I am shooting stars and
radiant nights and fireworks and explosions and
waterfalls and reindeer and bells and hydrogen
bombs and laughter and color and meaning and
clarity and joyousness and triumphant music and
pinwheels on the 4th of July and roman candles
and peace and quiet and noisy children and
orchestras and tympany drums and shouting and
loving and holding and caressing and kissing.
And know in your hearts ...

I'VE BEEN LOVING YOU FOREVER

A Message from Jakie

Jake is having an amazingly shitty day. She's so doped up on painkillers she can't quite make it to the bathroom. While I'm cleaning up, she notifies me in her sweetest, most darling little voice, "It's time to go to the hospital." I call her friend Shawn, who helps get her packed, and off we go. Jake doesn't make it through the night.

May 18, 2000. My precious sweetheart is gone and everybody is bringing corned beef sandwiches and cookies from Costco. I am crying so hard it hurts. In August, we would have been married twenty years.

My God, my life would have been so much easier if I only knew then what I know now—that I had been chosen to become a spokesman for the dead and bring forth wisdom from Spirit.

In the Beginning

Love! Regardless of what you think, or what they think. Love!
Even if you don't feel like it.

Another long, lonely trek down Sutton Street on a June gloom
kind of L.A. day. At Noble Avenue, the vintage BMW parked at
the curb is still for sale. This is the corner where Eli, Joe, and Bobby
risked their lives when they were little, attempting to navigate their
way to school against an endless onslaught of hostile and angry auto-
mobiles late for work.

I can still see Jakie filled with purpose, adorable in her shorts and
Lakers threepeat t-shirt, arm raised, coffee cup in hand, resolutely
stopping traffic long enough for the love parade of her chickens to
safely cross.

How many times did Jake intone her morning mantra, "Hold
hands crossing the street?" I reflexively put my hand down for an
imaginary little one to grab. Joe, ever the wise guy, would hold his
own hands. As they got older and played sports at the park, she also
became famous for, "Hold your balls in the parking lot," which always
got a laugh as everyone, myself included, grabbed their crotch.

The glorious scent of jasmine permeates the air. Our neighborhood is beautiful; the kids used to say it was "all bushy and treesy." It's lush, green and flourishing, and rustic with old-fashioned streetlights; the trees are incredible, especially the miraculous jacarandas with their mind-blowing purple blossoms. Gardeners, armed with noisy leaf blowers, swarm the neighborhood. Each lawn is proudly puffed up with distinctive vegetation; the flowers are varied and glorious. I've been walking this walk forever. I know it all: the remodels, the add-ons, the divorces, trophy wives, who's tented for termites.

What a splendid time it was when we moved into our home. The kids loved it, a classic California cottage on almost a flat half-acre, with a wonderfully romantic front porch. God, how the boys played and ran and squealed and wrestled on the land: the games, the races, the playoffs, the competition for champion of the world, the universe, running through sprinklers laughing their asses off on hot valley days, touch football, pickle, taking practice cuts in preparation for baseball tryouts. And hoops in the driveway. Hours and hours of hoops. Jakie was always out there horsing around with the kids. She had great hands and could run a buttonhook pattern with the best of them. Not much changed through the years—sure, the Jordan Jammer gave way to a wooden backboard over the garage, until Santa delighted everyone with a magical Plexiglas® one. Damn, it was so fun being a basketball family, especially during the height of the Lakers' Showtime run. After each thrilling victory, the Laker girls and the entire city partied to Randy Newman's, *I Love L.A.* From the freeways, to the mountains to the ocean, the sun was shining everywhere and we loved it!

Our life was homey, loud, loving, and above all else, entertaining. I had never known anything like it. Jake was our grown-up ringleader, setting up paddle tennis tournaments next door at the Dooleys', organizing firefly hunts, or excitedly yelling, "C'mon guys, I set a tent up outside and you get to camp out all night." The initial excitement and exhilaration was mind-blowing, but the kids never made it much past dusk. These city boys were scared witless. Maybe a squirrel would attack them?

Believe me, this chick Jake was a load of fun. You should have seen their faces as we approached "dead man's curve," driving in Topanga Canyon. She'd speak in her most ominous voice: "It was on a day exactly like today, exactly one year ago, at exactly this time, when a family exactly like ours, in a car just like ours, with kids named Eli, Joseph, and Bobby, managed to make it past the maniac's house, exactly like we did, but to no avail, because everyone ended up crashing in dead man's curve." Man, could she sell it. But what would you expect from a woman who honked in every tunnel—every time—on the way to the beach?

Memories float through my head as I stroll along. Like Jakie pounding perfectly timed air drumsticks, a mischievous look in her eye, to the throbbing drum solo in the middle of Bobby Darin's, *Beyond the Sea*. My eyes are drawn to the curb and I take in a piece of concrete that reads, "Eli Joseph Bobby Jake 1989." A tiny bit of existence. Incidentally, Jake's real name was Janet. Janet Kathleen. Her brothers called her J.K., which became Jake, and it stuck. The only time she was called Janet was when she was in trouble. "Janet, get in here!!!" Eventually, she became Jake legally.

I guess Janet and the gang couldn't resist the wet cement, and their fun and laughter left a memory for posterity. Jakie was here. We were all here. We will always be here. Yeah, right?

My god, how many times did we mosey down this enchanted trail together? Holding hands, getting away from the kids, pitching out story ideas for a script, or just floating along on balmy summer nights. And now, how many times have I taken these weepy strides alone, tears pouring down my cheeks, wondering why I didn't die with her? A young couple pushing twin strollers passes from the opposite direction. The husband nods and I burst out sobbing. God, I loved her so much. I wipe away the sweet-tasting tears and continue my lonesome journey, one step at a time.

Now What?

No one really knows how many years they have left. That's God's domain. Trying to figure it out is something like knowing which way the wind blows.

I'm defeated, depleted, deflated, and definitely screwed up. My back is killing me and I'm exhausted. I've been in shock ever since the day my lover was diagnosed. Saving Jake had been my all encompassing mission and I devoted myself to the caretaker role with all my heart. As far as relating to myself during that time, I was on automatic. I didn't matter. And now, in spite of all my efforts, she's gone. I'm stunned, let down, decompressing. My hyper, super-intense twenty-four-seven job screeched to an abrupt end.

Now what? What happens in real life after, "The End"? What happens in real life after the final credits roll and our precious life partner is dead and gone? We're left with a room filled with the artifacts of an existence. Drawers stuffed with socks, panties, and bras. Expensive sweaters from Bloomingdale's in dry cleaning bags. Pictures of children playing soccer, baseball, and basketball, holding trophies they don't deserve. Boxes and boxes of dust-covered trophies for being on the Reds, the Wizards, the Bulls, and the Butt Nuggets. That's the parks and rec hoops team Jake coached into the finals, the year we both lost it with unexpected bursts of anger. We screamed at refs, argued with park officials, and were generally out of our minds and no one thought it odd. We were humans acting humanly, our mental health problems hanging out for the entire neighborhood to see. We lived and loved and screamed, drank too much, and had married people sex—that's with one leg stuck in the pajama bottoms so they're easy to find. Life was idyllic. Our children were young; we were healthy, broke, and ambitious. Life was bliss and it would never end.

Now what happens to my love story? Does it continue through space and time or has it become a tragedy? Doesn't the poor schlub of a hero have to trudge on, carrying the enormous weight of his grief and responsibility?

A nurse from the hospital woke me up at six this morning and asked if I wanted to come by and see the body. "Hell no!" That bag of bones isn't Jakie. Her soul, her spirit, her essence—whatever you want to call it—has moved on. I saw the difference in her eyes between when she was alive in there and when nobody was home. She's full-fledged Spirit now—loving, playing, and overlooking our lives. The part that lives on is back with God. At least, I hope that's the way it is.

I spend hours moseying down the lonely turf, where even perfect days are gloomy. Trust me, the old neighborhood isn't quite so glorious these days; it's definitely missing its glow. Lost in my sorrow and pity, I barely notice the life-affirming flurry of activity from all the contractors. What a joke. People keep building and redecorating as if they're going to live forever.

I never know when the tears are going to come. Lots of times, they're tears of joy—sweet, like the memories that bring them on. If someone had told me going in, when I first met Jakie, that it would only last this long and I'd suffer this much, you know what— I'd do it all over again. I would have taken half the time. I mean it. I also would have taken double the time, but that doesn't seem to be a choice.

It was on one of my lonely, solitary walks when an amazing miracle occurred. I had just passed Kevin McCarthy's house with its overgrown rock garden (he's the actor from the original *Invasion of the Body Snatchers* movie), when I heard Jake's voice.

"Michael." It startled me. I stopped and looked around. All of a sudden I began to feel woozy—I could barely keep my feet. I started to yawn, a huge clearing yawn.

"Jakie…?" I muttered. What the heck is going on? I heard her voice, as clearly as if she were walking next to me, speaking inside my ear. I shrugged it off, figuring I was hallucinating from the stress. She's dead, for godsakes.

"I'm here," she said. Whoa! Barely able to stand, I dropped to the dusty curb to take it all in. I closed my eyes and breathed. I had to relax. That's when I felt her presence surrounding me and filling me and through me. I was totally captured in her quintessence. My mind didn't get it, but it sure as hell felt like her—she was with me.

I thought, *This can't be happening.* "Michael, it's me." But it was. It was! You know how, when you've known someone intimately and you've walked beside them for a long time, you know their feel. You have a sense of who they are, their presence, their touch, their energy. You know the comfort, the essence, the core of a person. Well, that's what it was like. Jake was present, and I told my mind to be still so I could take it in.

Sitting there on the grimy road, I considered, *Hey, it's possible.* Maybe Elton John was right when he said life is like a candle in the wind and even after the flame dies, the smoke remains.

"Love me as a Light Spirit, as a radiant ember of living Light." Those were the next words I heard. I was flabbergasted. Puzzled. Numb. Yet I could feel this energy. It was so…Jakie.

"I'm only going to be around for a short time, to set up some energy fields that will help you and the kids. Then I'll be moving on," she informed me matter-of-factly. I continued to take it in for as long as I could, but finally I blurted out what was most on my mind.

"Honey, I miss you so desperately. Do you miss me as much as I miss you?" I asked plaintively. I guess by then, I had stopped questioning if I was making this up, because I wanted so much to believe it.

She replied neutrally, "We don't miss here. Michael, it's glorious without the heartbreak of human love." I sat there and a smile broke out all over my face. It was so familiar, and we began to do what we always did—talk, talk, talk. We started having our usual intimate conversation; sure, it was inside my head, but somehow it stopped being strange.

"I loved you so much, honey."

"Don't use the past tense. I am alive, Michael, alive. More alive then I ever was. Love me in my new form."

"How? How?"

And suddenly, epiphany broke through the clouds and I got it. Jake didn't die; she simply moved on to her new home and is now more glorious, more potent, and more loving than she was in the flesh. She is pure pragmatic power. My god, she is still alive. She didn't die. You don't die. No one dies. Jakie lives. I started to scream and run down the block.

"Yes. Yes. Yes!!" Knowing this—I mean, really knowing it, feeling it, experiencing it—makes me feel so fantastic, so joyful, so comforted. I am deliriously happy. I don't have to dwell on the final days. I want that sadness out of my head. Jake wasn't the feeble, emaciated body that turned on her. She is a burning ember of radiant Light. That is what I will focus on. My love story continues.

Ah, to Be Young and Dumb

When you register grieving as completion, it opens the heart. Register it as healing, along the lines of a good cry. Like, it's about to rain. Try and stop the rain.

Life was perfection back in the day, certainly as excellent as my life could get. It's amazing how much inner pain the love of a good woman and a houseful of fun, screaming kids can cover up. I was happier than I could've ever imagined. That's a pretty profound statement from someone whose life had been pretty miserable and dark, until the day I got that job.

I smile as I recall the fateful moment when Jim Mulligan hired me as executive story consultant on the short-lived Norman Lear sitcom *In the Beginning*, starring McLean Stevenson. I showed up at the KTTV studios with my long hair, humming Lynyrd Skynyrd's, southern rock classic, *Free Bird*, when they told me to see some character named Jake about my parking space. I expected a dissipated, worn-out, old showbiz coot, not a twenty-four-year-old, beautiful blond California cheerleader with huge, loving, fun blue eyes and a killer body, wearing green painter pants and a red plaid flannel L.L.Bean shirt. Jake always had style. Admit it, how many women could pull off wearing high-top sneakers to a wedding and still look sexy and great? She did. And as an aside, Jakie's Converse All-Stars lasted longer that Walt and Janet's marriage.

One look and I was a goner. I had found my person; I finally found my love. It was so weird and wonderful—our vibes were so intense that I was almost compelled to put my hands all over her in the Xerox room. Of course I didn't, but I swear, I had to force myself to hold back. I wasn't a pervert, but she must have felt it too, because within a week we were lovers and my marriage and her current relationship were history. Then, as the months went by and we got past the instant attraction phase, I happened to notice she had a pretty face and was smart, funny, and sweet.

Jakie always mused that "sitcom people lead sitcom lives," and we fit the bill. Our program would have been called *The Wacky Weinbergers*, starring Jake as the sweet, sexy, hardworking mom. I am the irritated, angry, narcissistic dad. Eli plays the role of the buttoned-down Michael J. Fox from *Family Ties*. Joey's the impish, mischievous Kirk Cameron from *Growing Pains*. Bobby is the adorable toddler who gets along with everyone, until you push him too far, at which time he tries to take your head off with his little baseball bat. And David is the guest star—the child from the first crappy marriage, the blended family kid with all the hilarious anger that brings up.

Life was a boundless, fun-filled extravaganza, a magnificent, entertaining spectacle without a moment's peace and quiet. Sometimes to get away, Jakie would sneak up, grab me, and lock us in the bathroom. She'd have the wine uncorked and the good crystal Bordeaux glasses set up on the toilet. We'd make love on bath mats to the uproar of kids fighting, hitting, screaming, and laughing outside the door. Sometimes, we'd just sit on the floor, sip, and talk.

I guess we could have been intimate after the kids went to sleep, but we were usually too damned tired. We'd lie in bed, so close, face-to-face. She'd say, "I hope the kids don't walk in and find us dead from inhaling each other's carbon monoxide." That line was always good for a laugh. She was funny, too. Imagine—pretty, sexy, loving, smart, and a sense of humor. I never experienced anything close to the bliss I shared with Jakie.

My god, the tales she told, my Sheherazade of Sherman Oaks. Her Irish gift of gab kept me riveted, regaling me with "A Thousand and One Suburban Nights"—the adventures of her life, her childhood—bewitching me with honesty and a devilish humor, freely revealing the depth of her soul, holding back nothing.

A drummer dad and a lounge singer mom raised her with a cowboy mentality. She alleged, "Me and my brothers were put outside in the summer and were allowed to come back home in the winter. If we survived." She was a latchkey kid long before the term was coined.

While she was growing up, Jakie was a delectable tomboy surfer girl, following her brothers Chris, Tracy, and Tim everywhere. Like the time they took her exploring the new homes under construction in Tarzana. The cluster of tract homes was being built on tiers cut out of the rustic mountain. From a distance, the development looked like a giant staircase. At the top of the mountain, her brothers coerced her, since she was the youngest, into rolling a large rock down the hill. She did so gleefully, and watched in horror as it rolled down one tier...picked up steam...hit the front of a house...disappeared for a second...then crashed out the back and kept on going—in the front...out the back...tier after tier...in the front...out the back. As they ran away, she said, she laughed so hard she peed her pants.

She'd kill to retrieve foul balls at the brothers' Little League games for a free snow cone. She tagged along with them to the beach and became an excellent surfer until, "One summer, my boobs exploded and threw off my center of gravity." She wrote a letter to The Monkees inviting them to her birthday party and was traumatized when they didn't show up. She showed me a letter she received from President

Kennedy thanking her for suggestions on how to run the country. At least someone important had the decency to respond.

I know all about her mad crush, when she was attending UCLA, on a boy who turned out to be gay. Even after she found out, she blindly followed him around. "I was like Adele H. in the movie of the same name, hopelessly in love, a pathetic camp follower."

I still get ticked off thinking about how she got screwed out of making cheerleader at Reseda High, a position she was eminently qualified for. She was a lock, a knockout with golden hair, the quintessential California girl who was more enthusiastic and more athletic and could jump higher than anyone. She had been practicing for a year and was totally pumped for tryouts. Then on the fateful day, she got so excited she used the popular student adaptation of the cheer, "*Kill Kill Kill*," rather than the administration-approved version of, "*Win Win Win.*" She was disqualified and devastated.

I know everything on her resume. Her stint as an impeccable gift wrapper for that cheap bastard who kept her tips, helping her mom do budgets for Procter & Gamble commercials, getting fired as Louise Lasser's personal assistant because she wouldn't work on Thanksgiving. I'm aware of the discord in her family—her brothers' fights, their run-ins with authority, her stepfather's affair, and how he once dragged Jake up a flight of stairs by her ponytail.

Jake's life was revealed in charming vignettes. They began in her cute apartment on Agnes Street, which was named for her great grandmother, who was married to the guy who worked for the people who named the streets. Then, as we grew bolder and we started venturing out to safe places where we thought no one would spot us, her story unfolded. Chinatown was our first stop. Who would run into us there? Besides, "It's Chinatown, Jake." Which reminds me—she was a very talented natural writer, even if we didn't know it at the time.

Jake's Grand Adventure

There is One who knows and guides you. The opportunity is to deepen the trust within yourself and with the One who walks with you.

When I started calling friends to share my misery, they were shocked, since most of them had no inkling about the severity of her "little" condition. We didn't go public with the news of "Jake's grand adventure," because that's the way Jake wanted it. She had no intention of burdening people or taking on their fear. She had no desire to spend her precious remaining time answering questions like, "How's your latest scan? Is the tumor growing, any new spots?" We didn't live in the realm of cancer specifics. That wasn't our focus. Our focus was living, not dying, and we pulled it off.

In the early days of her treatment, Jake and I laughed about developing a movie called, *Hiding Cancer.* The log line goes thusly: A husband and wife, always struggling as a writing team, finally get their big break when *Pow!* the beautiful wife is diagnosed. What to do? They run around town, pretending she's fine and when she can no longer hide the disease, they find a look-alike. They are never discovered because the shallow, narcissistic, self-absorbed denizens of Tinsel Town can't see beyond their own noses. Like they say, write about what you know.

People drop by in the sweetest way to pay their respects. I cry all the time, with every hello, on every phone call. I couldn't care less what people think. I go for long, weepy walks in the neighborhood and reflect on my kids. Joey is a man. Anytime I go off track, he's right there, taking care of me. He's beautiful and powerful. I have nothing to worry about with him. Eli and Bobby are working through their pain. They're all way more mature than I ever was. Jake and I did a first-class job.

The love Jakie created in her brief life is beyond me. Jakie loved people; she saw their Light, their goodness, and now, in return, there is a great outpouring of love and affection for her. I never realized how many wonderful friends we have. I guess you don't pay attention to mundane stuff like that when things are going well. Harvard-Westlake School is a wonderful community. The basketball coach sent a beautiful note from the Wolverines and I cry every time I read it.

One afternoon, after sharing a lox platter lunch at Solley's with Eli, I discovered a surprise on the fireplace mantle. Some living angel left an envelope overflowing with hundred dollar bills to help us out, with an unsigned note that read, "Because your angel is starting her new job." I broke out in sobs. I felt so loved. It was startlingly, amazingly, out of this world. The caring for Jake's family—that's me and the kids—is stupendous. People are calling and offering to help in incredible ways. We're the recipients of a colossal torrent of thoughtfulness and food. I have never experienced such an unbelievable show of warmth, compassion, support, humanity, and kindness. We have three or four dinners we can't get to—chili, lamb stew, Greek meatballs, and enchiladas. Hearty food is good. It gives us strength.

As I ponder my lot, my intention is to launch the next chapter of my love story, but there's still plenty of crap from the last chapter to be handled. Death-related junk, like taking care of insurance stuff, Writers Guild stuff, what to do with her residuals and pension, credit card stuff, legal death certificate stuff. Mucho grim shit.

Conversation Number Two

We're all constantly receiving a treasure chest. It's time for us to open it and own what's inside.

I spoke with a friend, a psychic chiropractor, who purports to see into invisible realms. I told him about my incredible experience of Jakie's spirit appearing and talking to me. He said it was absolutely true and advised me, if I wanted to have a better connection, she would come closer if I ate and drank her favorite foods. Especially since she was so recently departed.

Sure enough, as I increased my tequila, Cabernet, and lamb chop intake, our long-distance conversations intensified. We spoke loads of times, and it was always divine. Her loving energy pervaded me, her impression lingering like a waft of perfume hanging in the air long after the woman is gone.

I've read accounts of tales from beyond and phone calls from the dead, seen TV shows about people contacting loved ones who died, but I was always skeptical. "C'mon everybody, let's have a séance and see what Grandma's up to?" Why? Grandma gives me the willies. But my perception has changed; I've had the experience. I accept these conversations as true, but I keep an open mind. Maybe they're simply made up out of my wishful thinking? I guess that's possible, but I don't think so. However, I won't be able to absolutely prove their validity until my time on this strange planet is up. I'll let you know then.

Friday May 20. Jake has been gone from Planet Earth for two days. I'm lying in bed meditating, propped up on the expensive down pillows we splurged on at Bloomy's. Suddenly, a blissful energy overcomes me and I am comforted and complete, filled with Jakie's presence—as all-encompassing as when we were young, when I couldn't get her touch off me. Not that I wanted to. Wow, she was delicious then and she is delicious now. I remember when we first started dating, an act as simple as putting on my socks would cause me to moan, "Jakie."

My eyes still closed, I turned to the subject at hand and inquired, "Jake honey, is that you?"

"Yes, Michael."

Oh man, this is so cool. This is going to be some expedition. I couldn't decide if I was the saddest or the luckiest man alive. But I'm also a practical man, so I decided to use our time together wisely. I may be crazy, but I'm not stupid. If I'm making this stuff up, so be it. It feels so good.

"Can I ask you a few questions?" I asked.

"Yes, Michael."

Good. I had prepared for this moment, even though I wasn't sure it would ever come. My plan was to keep my tape recorder—the one we used in our story meetings—nearby, ready to hit record. I spoke my questions out loud and repeated everything I heard her say inside my head. That way, I could let the Panasonic do its magic, so I wouldn't have to write anything down.

"Did anyone meet you in Spirit when you died?"

"All the spiritual teachers through the ages, including Jesus," Jake shot back. "Current spiritual teachers, too. They're doing brilliant work. I love and appreciate them all."

That made me smile. Jake and I had consciously been studying spirituality for a long time and we've been initiated into a line of energy that encourages a devotion to the God within. A devotion to Spirit, to returning to our home—the soul—from which we originally came before we incarnated onto this earth, to rise into the heart of God. Which I'm sure is where Jakie is today.

"Does prayer matter? It sure didn't seem to help you when you got sick." *Got sick?* What a choice of words. She had colon cancer, for godsakes.

"Yes and no. It can't override what's to be, but no love is wasted. And remember, no one passes from this life unless the higher self and the soul agree to leave. It's all perfect."

"Does it matter that people love you?"

"Yes, big time."

"I'm planning a memorial service for you. Do you want anything special?"

"Nope, it's for the living." Hmmm, that makes sense. She's already pure glory, but I sure as hell could use some nurturing.

"Is it okay people give me money because you're dead?"

"Cool, all you can get."

"I'm having a hard time taking from friends, but I need it so much," I whine. All of a sudden, I'm back in my human self, feeling sad and let down.

"Oh God, accept it, Michael. Receive God's blessings. Those checks are God's blessing for you. It's not from people. That's God blessing you, telling you your burdens are done. You are free of debt. You are no longer indebted. Take the money; take the blessing. It's a blessing from God. And at the memorial, thank the people for their charity and ask them to continue it in little ways every day. It opens the hearts of the people who give and opens the hearts of the people who receive. It makes the world a little softer." Ain't that the truth?

"Are you dead, honey?" I blurt out.

"No!"

"What do you think of your death experience?"

"I'm not dead, Michael. I am engaged and alive, more than you can imagine."

"Will I join you eventually?"

"Yes. Eventually everyone will." Well, that's a comforting thought. I pressed on for more information.

"Do you want a memorial ad in the trades?" That's the showbiz trade papers, *Variety* and *The Hollywood Reporter*.

"I couldn't care less."

"Is there anything you want me to tell anyone else?"

"Yes, tell everyone to love me as a Light Spirit, as an angel, as a burning ember of living Light. Tell the people at the service that life goes on, on earth and in other realms and other dimensions. And God *is* the joy and loving that has come forward for our family. And everyone should honor the God inside themselves as a way of honoring Jakie. The God in Jakie is the God in you and we are all blessed to come together to know this. Give everyone the freedom to love. All is forgiven." Oh wow, that's so beautiful. She's a really great writer. Why did I argue with her so much when we were working on scripts together?

"What if I go out with someone?" I meekly and hesitantly queried.

"Honey, you live on earth; you're entitled to exchange your energy with a woman. It doesn't affect me at all."

"Why do I feel so guilty when I think about dating someone else?"

"Because I trained you so well."

I laughed. She still has great timing and a wonderful sense of humor. God, I miss her. No one cracks me up like she can. "I have to ask again 'cause it's bugging me," I pressed on. "People want to pay to get us out of debt. Is that okay?"

"I told you. It's wonderful, makes things easier on you and the boys. It's God's way, God giving to God. God is taking your burdens, taking your pain. Let whoever wants to help, help. Take it in. It's love. See all those bills gone. And don't ask me again."

"Eli had a big cry today and—"

At that moment, guess who sticks his head into the bedroom? It's that wonderful, handsome child, Eli. Perfect timing.

"Hey, E, guess who I'm talking to right now?"

He shrugs, "I don't know."

"Mom."

He takes a beat, rolls his eyes, looks at me like I'm crazy, mulls it over for a while and finally asks, "What's she doing?" I know Eli's response seems a little odd, but you have to take it in the context that his parents have spent the last sixteen years exploring spiritual matters and he's used to us being oddballs.

"I'm having so much fun, Eli. Lighthearted fun, like skipping and playing and laughing," she tells him.

He doesn't react much—maybe because he's numb from everything that's been going on around here lately, or maybe because Jake and I were so weird through the years. He finally responds, "Do you miss us?"

"I know you have expansive love for me, Eli, but we don't miss here; we just love. My love is no longer directed at you. Now it encompasses you. As I told Michael, don't love what was here. Love what's here now and you'll be with me."

"How come I wasn't home for a long time when you were sick?"

"Well, sweetheart, it was more important for you to complete the semester on time. It's part of your path and you couldn't have done anything to help me, because it was a done deal. Michael said you were being sad today, so take that sadness now and place it into the Light. The energy of God is here right now; I'm bringing it to you and it will lift your sadness and relieve you of that. Breathe. It's just your mind; it's just your guilt and your sorrow; it's not you, Eli. You're so much grander than that. You were the perfect child to me when I was your mother. You lifted my heart to where I am now and gave me great joy, which I carry forward in my work today."

That's so sweet. I started to cry.

"You finally have a job? You never worked all that much here," Eli joked. And it was an expensive joke, too. What can I say? Comedy writer couples make funny kids. "What did you do today?" Eli pushed on.

Jakie laughs. "There was a seminar in this land of—and you won't understand this word—Oobaloch or something like that. It's a place where we learn greater mysteries of Spirit that don't translate to human form."

"Is there time where you are?"

"No. Joey would love it here. It's just being. It's a radiant, dynamic, energetic, static sense of knowingness, beingness. In earth terms, it's constantly dynamic and fulfilling." Jakie laughs again. "I know who you are, Eli, and I invite you to know who I am."

"Who are you?"

"A radiant ember of living Light," she repeats. Damn, so that's it. She's an exploding firecracker in heaven.

"How long will you be with us—able to talk to us?"

"I don't know. I have some personal work with Michael. This conversation is for you. There won't be many more. You know your job—your work—and don't worry about anything. The Spirit of God is pouring through our family; you are protected. It'll just carry you along, Eli."

"Anything I need to do?" asks Jake's most precious firstborn.

"You'll know. You'll know. I can't tell you; it's your process. You'll find out. You'll figure it out. That's part of this puzzle. That's part of the joy. It's an unfolding process, Eli; you're a young man. Here's a human thing I can tell you. When I was there with you, I adored you with perfect perfection and you lifted me and changed my life. I bless you and you are blessed. There's a blessing going on right now. Take it in."

And the room started to fill with an energy reminiscent of Eli's first meal at his mother's breast. It was so beautiful. Eli and I hung in the silence for a short, sweet time. Then Jake turned her attention back to me. "Michael, get over this as fast as you can. There's work to be done." What kind of work? What are you talking about? I'm just an ordinary guy who feels like crap most of the time.

And with that, she faded away. Eli and I looked at each other. Was it real or was it Memorex? Who knows, but, holy cow, was that cool!

It Was All Her Fault

As you begin to love, your health and happiness will grow.

She started it. I didn't force her to plop herself down in my office with that jug of wine. Yep, it was her fault. At least until the next night, when I took her to Lucy's El Adobe for margaritas. Man, could the girl flirt. And drink. My prayers had been answered. Jake was my heart's desire, a drinking buddy with boobs.

We laughed and talked and yearned. I was dancing inside. When they started putting chairs up, I got the hint it was time to walk her to the parking lot. That's where I kissed her for the first time. And she kissed back. Life is good. Immediately risking my marriage, I suggested we go back to her place. She said, "Not possible," so we called it a night. Later, she admitted, "I wanted to invite you over, but my apartment was messy." I guess cleanliness is next to godliness, but you'd think with all her smelly brothers, she'd know I couldn't care less.

However, it wasn't long before she straightened up the place and I was welcome. She opened her screen door wearing a pair of Levi cutoffs with just a hint of butt cheek showing and something cute on top, which I can't remember, because I was so taken with her legs and the promise of where they met. I think I impressed her, because I brought over two bottles of champagne and two bottles of wine—one red, one white—just in case. Not to mention a Van Morrison and Beatle LP. Maybe I was a little over the top, but before the night was over, we were lovers and I was paying her rent.

We were out of control, insane, mad for each other love. With a capital L O V E. It was a major rush and we were totally honest, open, and free with each other. Let's get real—neither of us expected this cool, sexy fling to go anywhere. Jake said, "This is good. No games. We'll just have fun and be friends; we don't want anything from each other, because I have a boyfriend and you have a wife." Sure, bet?

On our second date, still at her house because I was afraid to go out in public, she charmed the pants off me, literally, by lip-syncing, the Beatles' "I'll Get You" (and she did!), wearing only a faux fur coat and a pair of roller skates.

Damn, I was smitten. We were having so much fun laughing and talking and listening to records. She told me I was "dead meat" and she was correct. Soon, we were sneaking around, going to out-of-the-way places like the Coral Beach Cantina, a Mexican dive high up in Malibu.

After a pitcher of margaritas, I dropped a quarter in the oldies jukebox and we started dancing real close. I sang along with *You Send Me*, garbling the words as Sam Cooke serenaded us with something about getting married and starting a home.

She said, "What?" I started to tap dance. "You can't take it back, you can't take it back."

True to the gospel of Lennon and McCartney, my life was *Getting Better* and better since Jake was mine. Our attraction was intense, crazed. I raised the stakes and we took off for Palm Springs, where we didn't leave our room at the Canyon Hotel for thirty-eight straight hours. When we finally ventured into the 116-degree desert air, we could barely walk. At the pool, she dove off the high diving board with an elegant and exuberant athleticism that made every man envious. As she did laps, I was so happy she loved me back.

Later that evening, she sent me down to the hotel's fancy restaurant by myself. She arrived fifteen minutes later and asked the maître d' if a Mr. Weinberger had arrived yet. She sauntered over and slipped into my booth, pretending to be the highest priced call girl in the world.

The next night, to impress her back, I took her to the clam bar at the Hungry Tiger. I ordered a super-expensive combination plate of all kinds of raw clams and oysters. We wolfed them down. It wasn't until much later that we both admitted how much raw shellfish disgusted us. We only ate it to impress each other. Ain't love grand?

Unfortunately, our "friendly" arrangement was too good to be true. Sure enough, she broke up with me after a few weeks, because she was falling in love and didn't want to get hurt. I moped around like a lonely teenager, reminiscent of high school when Toni Benvenutti decided to just be "friends," and there would be no more groping to, "Don't be shy, don't even sigh, for you are my guy, you are my guy."

This was worse. I was supposed to be mature by now, but my emotions were in shambles. I had Jakie all over me. I was worse than a pimply high school kid with his first crush, tingling with desire. I was pitiful. Thank god she was pathetic, too, and couldn't hold out. I can't tell you how delighted I was when RKO Studios called less than an agonizing week later. That was our secret signal that we had to talk and since RKO was defunct, we thought we were so clever. She caved, a victim of love, agreeing to take me as I was. Adele H. lives. Thank god.

Before you could say, "I'm getting a lawyer," we were living in our little love shack on the beach in Malibu. I was having probably the greatest midlife crisis known to man. We played, drank too much wine, made love, and laughed. Totally absorbed with each other, we were riveted, enthralled, captivated, immersed, fascinated.

Life was a blast, but all too quickly Jake developed a serious side effect to our earth-shattering love affair: pregnancy. Holy shit!! There go those wild and crazy days. She quit smoking and drinking overnight. Always ahead of her time, she looked great jogging around Malibu, her sweet protruding belly leading the way. She did pregnancy quite stylishly. In fact, when she showed up at the hospital with ferocious contractions, she looked so fine in her jogging shorts, they didn't believe she was pregnant and tried to send her home. They thought she was some kind of crackpot. How cute is that?

Life through Jakie's expectant months was still fun and exciting, but we had one small problem—my divorce, or rather the lack of it. It wasn't happening. The legal proceedings were acrimonious, progress was stalled, and Jake's belly kept getting bigger and bigger. This was a predicament, because we preferred to honor the baby by being married before he was born. As the days rolled along, Jake came up with a brilliant plan. "I know. We'll hire an actor to play a minister and marry us for the family." I agreed; it was a dazzling proposal, and we put out a casting call to our out-of-work friends.

Ultimately, it wasn't necessary. We managed to get hitched two full months before Eli officially joined the clan. In that stretch, I think I was single for a total of six days. As a not unexpected side note, Jakie made a sunny and radiant bride. To look at her, you'd barely notice that she was seven months gone.

Two months later, our first shared spiritual experience occurred when Eli was born. Quite possibly, it was the defining moment of our lives, perhaps all the lives of our total existence. After a short time in the baby holding area, Eli, who didn't have his name yet, was brought in for his first meal. As Jake took him in her arms and he began to nurse, the energy around us shifted dramatically. The air started to shimmer and glisten, almost glow. Jakie sparkled as we felt the palpable, thick sweetness of her loving radiate into all of us, through the gift of her nourishing breast. It was a freakin' religious experience. At that moment, it was as if we were transported to a higher, more beautiful realm. Fantastic. Heavenly. Pure.

"Do you feel it too?" She nodded, cradling her baby and smiling from her soul. The way I look at it, Eli was the little chap who turned on the tap that allowed Jakie's boundless love to flow into the world, where it continues to this day.

That night, with her beloved in her arms, Jake fulfilled her transformation from wild, fun-loving adventuress to loving, nurturing mom. Our rock-and-roll days were a thing of the past. She was twenty-seven and had only eighteen years to live.

Conversation Number Three

Experiencing Spirit is like surrendering into the awareness of snow falling, the beauty of winter snow at Christmastime, the quality of hush, the silence in the snow.

As I was lying listlessly in bed, which I seem to be doing about twenty hours a day, I started yawning a really big involuntary yawn, which is usually a sign that Jake is in the neighborhood. My mouth stretches open and my face distorts, and this process can last a full five or ten seconds. When my mouth finally closes, I experience her presence as Jakie swoops in on a sweetness, a preciousness, a knowing.

"Hi, sweetie-pie," I welcome her. My fingers are crossed.

"Michael," Jakie laughs, "you're doing really, really, really well. You know, if I didn't know better, I'd come back and reincarnate and love you all over again." At last, the lovers speak.

"Yeah, I'm so proud of my family," I add.

"You guys are freakin' awesome." Only, she didn't say freakin' and I wondered if all angels curse in heaven, or do they just do it when they're on assignment? But I didn't ask; I had bigger fish to fry.

I asked about my most pressing concern and queried, "Do you have anything specific to tell about work?" Before Jake got diagnosed, work and money were what I usually worried about. Then, I started worrying about work, money, and her health.

"There's nothing for you to be doing. It's all lined up. The days just have to go by. Maybe you could get your teeth fixed in the interim." My teeth! Damn. I still have this goofy dental appliance I got in Switzerland when I had my root canals pulled because I had nothing better to do, and I need to find a holistic dentist, and I have too much on my plate. Oh, the trip to Switzerland? That's where we went for the cure after the doctors here gave up on her. But that's a whole other story.

"Do you have to reincarnate?"

"No. Where I am is pure Spirit fields."

"Was it worth it, everything you went through?"

"Absolutely."

"Oh Jakie, I miss you so much. It feels a little empty inside." There I go again, Mr. Whinyhead.

"Honey, don't be so hard on yourself. That's the physical bonding part between us. We were so close, it was as if our cells merged and our skin has to be separated. You feel it; I don't. I don't have skin. I've been liberated from that condition."

"Yeah, there's sure a part that overlaps and hurts."

"It's natural, like a scab being pulled off. It hurts because you're switching from our physical bonding to being complete within yourself. Time will heal it."

What!! Be complete with myself? Be real. How the hell am I going to pull that off? It's too much to consider, so I change the subject to one I often use to distract myself.

"Girls?"

"The sooner you see someone, the sooner you'll get a little comfort. Remember, in terms of the woman thing, I'd be aggressive, but I wouldn't forget about foreplay. You're not married anymore. Go slow."

Hey, my foreplay is fine. "What do you do on a date?" What a stupid question. I mean, I know, but it has been a long time. I am a faithful man. At least I was with Jake.

"You goof, take someone to dinner. Give them wine. See if they invite you over. If they don't after three times, don't go out with them anymore! That's the rule. You deserve a good time. There are several women, at the moment, who are right for you. You'll meet them soon."

"Do all angels pimp their husbands?"

"What comes forward in your life, Michael, is for your growth, your comfort, and the joy in God. My job in heaven is the joy in God. Just like your job will be, and is, the joy in God. You're to be happy, to have joy, in the midst of apparent sadness. You're to lift people's awareness in terms of death. Write your experience. Keep it fun. And marry someone wonderful, happy, and rich."

Wow, wowee! A directive from Spirit. I'm supposed to be happy and talk about death. I get to tell people you don't die. Hmmm, not an easy task, but I'll give it a shot. I'll sit at the computer and if I get stuck, I know who I can turn to for help—my old writing partner.

Then for good measure Jakie adds, "Tell everyone dying is not a failure. I didn't do anything wrong. I didn't have to accomplish more in my life. What I went through is a natural progression. Endorsed by the Spirit."

There you have it, Mike. That's the job. To turn Jake's death into a positive for myself and others. It's not going to be easy; I've still got plenty of grieving ahead of me.

Twenty Years Ago Today

Lay claim to something you don't know exists. But claim it anyway. To be happy, start acting like you're happy. What do happy things look like? Declare yourself happy.

Jake took to motherhood like a priest to an altar boy. It was her calling. The more she loved Eli, the more she loved me, the more she loved Eli, and on and on. Life was serene. We'd dig a hole on our beach, stick Eli in it, and talk and plot.

It wasn't more than six months or so before Jake was back in shape, her stomach flat and those few extra expectant mother pounds gone. No doubt, she was looking as sexily splendid as the day we met and next thing you know, that reoccurring side effect showed up. She was pregnant with Joe.

With another one on the way, we needed a bigger place, so we bade goodbye to the beach and moved to the Valley. Soon it was Joseph's turn to be born. What a disaster! He was massacred, his skull fractured because of a high forceps delivery administered by an impatient doctor. What a way to enter the world—roughed up, yanked around, and dragged through a hole half your size. What was that prick doctor thinking? I should have sued his ass. Believe me, it's pretty tense having your kid born with a bloody eye, a lot of suffering, and a lot of fury.

But Joe was a toughie and he healed up pretty fast. And on the positive side, his ordeal started a small set of congruent miracles that led to us finding our spiritual path.

Joseph spends a few extra days in the hospital healing up, and when he comes home, Jakie now gets to juggle a newborn and a sixteen-month-old. Jake always said, "One kid's a hobby; two's a job." Boy, did her job kick-start. It was a tough time. She was dog tired, empty, and worn out, yet she kept on going, like Marlon Brando after he was shot five times in *The Godfather*. Her favorite statistic, which she loved repeating, was, "Of all the women in the world raising two children under two, one hundred percent of them are depressed."

To reward her for working her tushie off, I'd serve her breakfast in bed and play her favorite movie, *The Quiet Man*, on the VCR. I'd kiss her and her eyes would sparkle and we'd be lovers all over again. And then a kid would scream and that would be that.

We were pretty broke, since I had alimony and child support payments, and I took every job in sight. That's when Jake started to help out on my scripts. So here she is, overwhelmed, in the throes of motherhood, and now I've got her writing with me. She put her foot down. "We'll hire a nanny first and then we'll pay for food." I agreed.

Through it all, Joseph's birthing boo boo kept him irritated as hell. All the doctors could promise was he'd feel better eventually. Thanks so much. But Jake wasn't going to let her baby boy suffer—that's not her nature—so she began her quest to get him some help. After a bunch of dead-end leads, Jakie spoke to her mom, who saw this masseuse, who knew this chiropractor—and since I didn't believe in anything other than the Beverly Hills Hebrew medical establishment—she pulled a Jakie on me and sneaked Joe out, like she was taking him to Lourdes. He got his first treatment and amazingly, the crying stopped a little bit. He was definitely improved, so I went to check out this chiropractor chick.

I liked Hedy; I got a few treatments myself, and before you could crack a back or lift a lumbar, Jake and I were studying, "The Teachings of the Spiritual Heart," a set of discourses written by Hedy's spiritual teacher. The promise is, "As you begin your inner journey, you will be filled with joy and the glorious feeling of love." Sounds good to me.

Not to dwell, but plain-wrap spirituality appealed to me. It's non-denominational and you don't have to show up anywhere. I especially liked that it was a group filled with non-joiners and non-followers, following a non-leader. I definitely fit in. And it was practical. You didn't have to believe in anything—you either experienced it or not. Simple stuff like being responsible and taking care of yourself and others. I recognized the wisdom, but acting nice was new to me. I was brought up with *the teachings of the greedy heart*—you know, get the other guy before he gets you, don't trust, and money is all that matters.

Jake was more in tune with the whole God thing and was grateful we found it, I think more for me. I admit it, I needed lots more spiritual softening than she did. Jake, who saw meaning in everything, believed that, "Joe was tough enough to get his head cracked open and he did it for us, so we could lift up our minds and begin thinking about cosmic love and concepts greater than ourselves. That was his gift."

Life? Go figure. In less than two years, I met my soul mate, participated wholeheartedly in a glorious, passionate rug burn brand of love affair, got divorced, and now I've got a mountain of bills and crying kids, and Jake and I have become full-fledged California nuts. How in God's name did this happen? Do you think maybe I wasn't paying attention?

Reality Sucks

Whistle when you put your shoes on.

I've been working round the clock getting everything cleaned up and organized. I started with her closet, offering her friends the first pick of all the adorable Jakie fashions, and then I gave the rest of her stuff to charity. Figuring out what to do with the expensive wig she had made in case her hair fell out from the chemo was really creepy and strange. Ultimately, her friend Shawn donated it to a women's charity.

Then I got onto the paperwork of cancer: file after file filled with doctor stuff, bills, blood tests, cancer research. I couldn't toss it quick enough. It sickens my stomach. And whenever I think everything's handled, an article of her clothing shows up—a sweater or something—and sets me off all over again. I cry all the time; I don't care where or when, it feels so damn good. Plus, my kids get to watch me and that gives them permission to express their pain.

Then there's my concern about money. At first, I had a hard time receiving, but after I talked it out with Jakie, it became easier. She told me the money's not from people, it's from God. Wherever it comes from, it sure comes in handy. I am as broke as I've ever been. We've been living on faith and fumes. It's a little humbling, yet receiving makes me feel so loved. I cry again, realizing that I am not alone. A famous couple, very dear to my heart, reminded me of that.

I didn't even pretend to work or do anything for the past year. We lived on credit. Christ, treatment in the cancer industry is expensive. I didn't care. Take my house, take everything, but not my wife, please.

I am so appreciative of the help, because I insist on paying off my huge debt, one hundred percent on the dollar. The credit card companies should be honored, not punished. They were there for me; they trusted me; they stood by me, fed me, paid for my kids' school, my mortgage, and Jakie's medicine and treatment. I know they don't know this, but they saved my life and tried to save Jakie, too.

I hate being alone, especially at night; all I do is watch TV and drink. The few times I didn't kick back a little vino, I didn't sleep at all. I have too much angst. My mind won't stop; I can't shut it off.

In bed, I toss and turn and reflect; everything moves in slow motion. I had a remarkable time with Jake in Switzerland. I had an awesome time this whole year. Believe it or not, it was a great year, in spite of everything—probably the greatest year of my life. I relished every second, great love, great fun, great sharing—not New Year's Eve kind of fun, but sweet fun. Jake and I were side by side for almost every precious second of her finale, at home with the family or vacationing in the Alps. Sometimes, we'd be sitting together and I'd get real close and just sniff her. I was blessed to have a soul mate and I smiled inside at our closeness.

Jakie went about dying in her unique way. At the end, she had the people around that she wanted, the people closest to her. She could have left earlier—she was sick enough—but I swear to God she waited for Eli to take his finals and then she gave him a little extra time to get used to the idea.

When the surgery was complete, we didn't tell the boys she had metastases. What good would it have done? They thought the cancer was gone. It wasn't. Plus, we sincerely believed we would win the fight. So, toward the end when they figured it out, they were a little pissed. However, more important, they had their healthy mom living inside of them a little longer. Would worrying a whole extra year have helped? What, was Eli going to fly home on weekends to watch his mom fade away, instead of living the raucous frat life at Duke?

I can't sleep. I get up, pour myself some more wine, and sit sadly alone in the living room, wondering why God pulls this crap.

The mood around here can change in an instant. We shoot from total black depression to euphoric amazement in seconds. Sometimes, my kids and I look at each other, because we feel so good, so blissed out that we wonder if we're going crazy. People are coming up to us and they're three days behind, "Ohhh, I am so sorry," and I go, "Yeah, I guess I am, but..." Jake's in a better place and she's out of pain. I can't tell you how good that makes me feel. It's a relief to have some respite from the caretaker role.

At the end it was pretty tough on her and it was grace that got her out of here so fast. It's funny: I can be elated for a second and then I'll glance at a picture of our younger days, slip into that cavernous, miserable aspect of myself, start missing her, and cry and cry. I hate those final scenes of Jakie, all skin and bones, going round and round in my head. I close my eyes and sometimes that's all I see, like a horrible car wreck happening over and over.

Spirit has given me the gift of awareness of Spirit in my life. Spirit "did" me in this process. It held me, taught me unconditional loving, sheltered me, comforted me, led me, and encouraged me.

To honor Jake and in the spirit of keeping it normal, I let the boys have friends over. It was so cute. The kids were all respectful and sweet as they held eye contact and hugged me. Then, after they had paid their respects, a bunch of them went into the living room and a beer party broke out. I had to break it up; I couldn't handle the noise. I wasn't mad—they came with such love. I hope they raised a brewski to toast Jakie before I kicked their sorry butts out.

There Are Places
I Remember

It's an awakening. We are all a consciousness of the Spirit. However, until the realization comes, it doesn't exist.

The early child rearing years are a blur. All I remember is mucho crying crying crying and mucho writing writing writing. Man, it flew by. Thank god we have photo albums to prove we were there. Yes, there is visual proof from the many rolls of film I shot, that Jake bathed the kids, over and over, in both the sink and the tub. I see that we ventured out to Chuck E. Cheese's, nursery school events, and David's school functions, even if I don't remember doing so. People say, "If you can remember the sixties, you weren't there." I say, "If you can't remember when your kids were little, you were there."

In the pictures, my honey and I look so numb and burnt out. Jake was consumed with little behinds. She changed every one of their diapers with love, a sweet smack on the tush, and a hearty, "You're good to go." We fell in love and got married because we wanted to be together and now we rarely see each other. She's exhausted and so am I from all the crazy writing staff hours. I miss her. Plus I need her. She helps me by typing my scripts, and when she hands them back, they're miraculously better. Sometimes I wonder if I put too much of a burden on her, but she's a strong, hardworking woman who'd do anything for her man. And do it cheerfully.

Tough times. We staggered through them as best we could. Our young lust led to over-creating a family and left us overcommitted, but damn, we still loved each other's face. We must have, because a few years later, Jake had a relapse of that pesky side effect. She was pregnant with Bobby. What were we thinking?

However, this time we got smart. We went for the combo deal. Jakie had a caesarean and her tubes tied at the same time. Yay!

Life became a blur of baths, diapers, jobs and more blur blur blur. More crying. More writing. And before you know it, the pressure eases a hair. Joe and Eli are in school and Bobby starts kindergarten.

It was around this time, when I came off a particularly demanding show that was cancelled, that Jake and I made a momentous decision. We decided to become writing partners. Officially. I missed her, she was talented, and damnit, she needed to get out of the house.

Hooray! Life was bliss again. I was living my dream. We were inseparable, together night and day, breathing each other's air. So what if we were broke? We grew even closer as we fought to make a living. It took a while, but after a few scripts, a few setbacks, and a few years, we were getting jobs and having fun. Weekends were spent at the park watching the kids play ball. We ate well, drank fine wine, fought, wrote, and made love. Jakie's eyes still sparkled, but she couldn't get pregnant anymore. There is a god.

She blossomed at work, becoming an excellent writer, confident and funny in the rewrite room. Was it any surprise that she could hold her own with all those powerful men? She loved guys and was as raunchy as the best of them. The twenty-four-year-old innocent had grown up, a product of all those details she lived that were now part of her writing expression: Like how to prepare the perfect peanut butter and jelly sandwich, keep score at baseball games, know that K means strikeout and 6-3 is short to first. Details like spitting on her hands to slick my hair down on the sides because she didn't like my wings, standing up to the teenage thugs who harassed a young Eli at the movies, baking cupcakes for school functions, throwing Thanksgiving dinners, standing in line at basketball sign-ups, arguing the merits of LBJ, writing absent notes, smoking a cigar with the menfolk, and putting up with me.

One job led to another, and soon we were selling pilots and working on shows like *The Tortellis, Saved by the Bell, Just the Ten of Us,* and *Growing Pains.* We were getting a little bit successful.

Showbiz. It's an amazing process. Jake and I were executive producers and creators of several produced television pilots, based on scripts we wrote. For each of these shows, the networks put up about a million bucks. Those few times we bordered on success were amazing. We were the belles of the ball. I was worthy; she was beautiful. People came out of the woodwork—flattering us, smiling, wanting to read every brilliant word we wrote, listening to us intently, writing down what I said, and calling me talented, a genius, and a reputable family man, too. It's a good thing my success was short-lived or I might have believed it. It seems that when you can offer someone a job in Hollywood, an ass is instantly presented with the flair of a sommelier displaying a fine wine, or sometimes with the subtlety of an Irish setter in heat.

To the uninitiated, it looked like people loved us, but it wasn't real love—twin soul love, unconditional love. It was ersatz; it had nothing to do with the heated, out-of-control attraction; the inability to get that incomparable person's touch off your skin; the pulsating, pheromone-sniffing, heart beating, exciting love that Jake and Mike felt when they came together and started a family. That's a love story for the ages— the true love of a simple man caring for his radiant wife as she carries his baby.

Personally, I was growing, too. In the PJ years—that's pre-Jake—I was loath to reveal myself, fearing that someone was watching and would get me. I hid in a protective pose, behind the armor of hyperactivity, alcohol, and sarcasm. I believed if anyone knew the true me, who I really was, they would hurt me. Beyond a doubt, it was only because of Jakie's love that I slowly became less paranoid and began to trust. It was one of her gifts.

Jake was just the opposite. She was liberated and open, immodest and direct. She always told the truth, even in ticklish situations that I would have found embarrassing. Her frankness amazed me. She was so natural; she never had an ounce of guile. No one ever gave of their love more freely.

So, here we are working our butts off, sixty-, seventy-hour weeks, choking in smoke-filled rewrite rooms until six in the morning. The kids are being cared for by a series of nannies—some excellent, some insane. Like Wendy, who would read them bedtime stories out of *The National Enquirer*, "The man with a hammer stuck in his head." Another winner, an archetype of idiocy from Denmark, used to scare Bobby by telling him they were lost and he'd never see his bed again. We put up with them because we had no other choice.

Finally, after two full seasons on staff, *Growing Pains* ended for us and we came home to find our children totally stressed out. I said, "Hey honey, notice anything about the brood? They seem a hair screwed up."

"I know," she replied impishly, "but I love their sorry butts, anyway." True, true. "What a surprise," she added amusedly. "I guess children need competent adult supervision after all." Bobby was down to about fifteen pounds; he didn't eat because no one fed him. Joey was out-of-control angry, and Eli was perfect. Too perfect, because he was the responsible adult in charge. At twelve. That was the moment of

Jake's next momentous decision. "As God is my witness, from this moment on, we'll work at home so I can be there for the kids. Sure, we'll make less money, but look around," she alleged, "don't the rich and famous people in Hollywood have the most sick and twisted kids in the world?" She put both feet down this time and declared, "Our children will not suffer from affluenza!"

So that's how we became poor, broke freelancers, writing at home and doing normal things again. Jake started fund-raising for their schools, becoming a master at organizing garage sales, while her Tetris scores soared on Joey's Gameboy. And she was still awe-inspiring at pitch meetings.

She loved the process of writing, and we would argue all the time about what worked and what was funny. Ultimately, she'd give in and let me think I had won. Oh, yeah? She did the inputting on the computer and therefore had the last pass. She did whatever the hell she wanted. Tricky, tricky.

We observed our family, and that's what we wrote about. One of my favorite projects was a feature script called *Breaking Joshie*, a comedy about a willful fourteen-year-old whose dream is to get free from his parents, which creates a titanic, humorous power struggle. The parents try everything to break Joshie, even sending him to "teen jail," a camp for incorrigibles. What Joshie learns there, besides finding out how powerful he is, is that the best way to get adults off your back is to give them what they want. He comes home, becomes an A student, joins all the honor societies, and—given the new freedom he earns— he throws the greatest illegal party of all time. Joshie never breaks.

We couldn't sell it. The studios hated it. They were appalled. Movie executives want well-behaved, pretend obedient kids in their flicks, because their own flesh and blood are such out-of-control losers. Our script was awesome, and real kids would have loved it.

More projects. More meetings. More pitches. Selling some, in production occasionally, striking out on others. We were house and tuition poor. The only constant was Jake looking hot and the kids thriving.

Jakie was Joe's bulldog. She'd make him sit at his desk for two hours every night and he would—doing nothing. He never broke. She was helping Eli get his college applications together and we were making it to most of Bobby's freshman basketball games, where he ultimately shared the team MVP. It was an angelic time. Jakie often mused, "Like a mole on Marilyn Monroe, I'm just happy to be here."

The fairy tale continued until, once upon a time, that goddamn day came, when my delicious, buoyant wife—the fun-loving mother of my kids, the ringmaster of the dazzling three-ring circus of our lives—was diagnosed with colorectal cancer. It was the saddest, most earth-shattering, gut-wrenching day of my life. Jakie was only forty-five.

She never had a symptom. We found out, out of the blue, during a routine gynecological exam a few days before Eli was set to graduate from high school. The medical whirlwind began. We went from one doctor to the next and the news kept getting worse. They said she needed surgery ASAP, but she insisted it wait. Eli was graduating.

That should have been one of the happiest days of Jake's life. And it was. She was so beautiful and courageous, beaming, as she watched Big E walk across the stage, pick up his diploma, and toss his cap into the air. She basked in his glory and was so proud that her firstborn was bound for Duke University in the fall. I was sick in my heart. Two days later, Jakie was in Cedars-Sinai Hospital having a large tumor cut out of her belly and slopped in a pail. As anesthetized as any patient, still not grasping, grappling to comprehend the gravity of it all, I nervously paced the eight-floor lobby, as a few friends tried to comfort and distract me. Finally, the surgeon appeared, way too early into the planned ten-hour surgery, wearing a tragically long face. It was too late. The cancer had metastasized.

I wailed and sobbed. This couldn't be happening. What was I going to do? There was no way I could live without her. We were attached at the hip. Two peas in a pod. She completed me. You never saw Mike without Jake or Jake without Mike, and we liked it that way. We shared one daily planner, one job, and one car. That's all we need-ed. We used to laugh and say, "Together we make one great person." Simply sitting next to her, feeling her presence, was heaven. We could read each other's minds. She thought about the kids and creating a home; I thought about sex and worried about money. I could feel her move through a room with my eyes closed. We raised codependency to an art form and were damn proud of it. We were lovers and still in love in spite of all the years. We adored our boys and were actively involved in every facet of their lives. Then, after an agonizing four hours of surgery, they sewed her up and said she had a thirty percent shot of lasting five years. Oh my god!

I was devastated, numb, the walking wounded. Sick and heartbro-ken, emptiness aching in the pit of my stomach, I moped and cried, but Jakie wouldn't have it. With tubes in her arms and a smile on her face, she meant it when she barked, "Hey, stop being a waste of skin. Buck up! We're going to have fun, *no matter what.*" We always did. For richer and most of the time for poorer. She wasn't going to allow us to stop now, even if our current "no matter what" seemed a little more urgent. We made a vow to enjoy and live our life to the fullest, even if she was dying. We toasted our resolve with a shot of Jose Cuervo. I drained hers and mine—since booze was no longer on her healthy, anticancer diet—and made plans for the future. Then I poured us another round.

Of course, I was bullshitting when I promised to enjoy myself through this ordeal. What was I going to do, tell her the truth about how hurt, fearful, abandoned, and inept I felt? Christ, do you think I was proud that inside my head, I was freaking out about how her dis-ease would affect me? Like I was the one with the problem. Sure, I lied to her. Who wouldn't? She had cancer, for Christsakes. But, be happy with what's going on? No way. This was easily the low point of what I considered a hurtful and accursed life, at least up until the moment I met Jake. I was in a deep, dark tunnel of depression with no possible light at the end. But I kept smiling.

Of course, I hadn't received her messages from beyond yet. I had no idea how happy she would be, by being dead—or how happy she wanted me to be, by being alive.

Out of Options

There is nothing unfair going on. Things are always going in a right and proper way.

After surgery, Jakie quickly regains her strength and those two goofy little cancer fighters, Mike and Jake, begin their quest. We've been best buddies before. We believed we spent tons of past lifetimes together, getting into trouble, making mistakes, and having a blast. We laughed and said we fell out of the Godhead and lost our way home. We were ready for the fight. It was second nature for us to hitch up our pants and look adversity in the eye. Hell, we were writers doing it for a living with producers, network executives, and agents. After showbiz, how hard could cancer be? C'mon, in Hollywood, sincerity is what gets you success, and when you've got that faked…

For the next six months, things went incredibly well. Jake got stronger and stronger as she became quite adept with her colostomy bag, the result of having a hunk of her colon cut out. She laughed and said that she had more time on her hands, since she didn't have to waste it going to the bathroom. Through it all, her cancer numbers stayed low. Her vitality returned. She was strong enough to be active with our sons at home, and to visit Eli in North Carolina and my mom in Florida. We even had a few business meetings. Jakie was always amused that she could be pooping into her bag during a story conference and no one would know it, but if you consider that we were television writers, that seems redundant.

During this entire episode, Jake only smiled. She was more peaceful and loving than ever, choosing to care for and focus on others, as I cared for her. She was active, fun, and upbeat. It might have appeared that she was keeping up a brave front, but she was truly cheerful, funny, and positive. There wasn't a doubt in her mind that she was going to beat the big C. She was living the spiritual teachings.

I worked like hell to buy into her positive attitude and optimism. This is what my honey-pie wanted and I gave it my best. It wasn't always easy, but I forced myself. But sometimes I would lose it, especially during those awful trips to all those depressing doctor's offices where the medical professionals look at cancer as a death sentence and pummel you with depressing statistics. Before Jake's illness, I didn't even know all those medical corporations existed. There are thousands of them. It's a whole industry, hidden in the heart of L.A., whose main purpose is not to save lives, but rather to provide an efficient roadway to the cemetery. It boggles the mind and pisses me off.

We were more or less back to our normal routine—getting the kids up, making brown-bag lunches, yapping at them to do their homework, going to Bobby's games, and listening to Joey talk about becoming a mogul in the record industry, while we leaned on him to stop throwing parties and cutting class. During this stretch of time, I did my most excellent best to avoid the seriousness of our adventure. I kept my fear under control by focusing on seeing her as radiant and healthy as the day we met. I tricked myself by supporting Jakie so intently, that I sometimes forgot my own depressing secret thoughts and the hollow feeling in the pit of my stomach. Besides, being with her still made me so happy. Things were going so well that we switched to a more upbeat and aggressive oncologist, who came up with a stronger protocol to wipe out the cancer for once and for all.

That's when the numbers turned—for the worse. New side effects showed up, not just the nausea from the time we spent in the chemo lounge, but unsettling goings-on, like a new microscopic spot on the lungs. It was spreading. We managed to stay positive, even when the good doctor called us into his office and hurriedly and horridly told us that there was nothing more conventional medicine could do and Jakie's only alternative was to go home and die. I did a double take and crumbled inside. "Go home and die"?

They've given up on her!?? What? She's still active and healthy. Holy shit! Other more intelligent and weaker people might have been discouraged, but not Jakie. No, sir-ee. When we told Dr. Soram Khalsa, the Beverly Hills M.D. who was lovingly monitoring the overview of Jakie's case, about our predicament, he advised in his most upbeat chirp, "Switzerland, baby."

We started to pack immediately. Ordinarily, it would have been impossible for Jake to leave the kids, because she was so devoted, but what choice did she have? In her typical lighthearted fashion, she told her friend Heide, "The kids'll be fine, but just in case, I'm leaving bail money under the sink."

Three days later, my sweetie and I were winging it on Swiss Air, paid for with all the frequent flyer miles I had acquired going into debt sending my kids to private school. Our destination was the Paracelsus Klinik in Lustmühle, Switzerland. This place touts itself as a champion of European biologic medicine. They say that rather than focusing on the cancer, their approach is to reestablish the body's own harmony to foster healing. Hope exists! The cure awaits. Let's get it on.

We put on our best face and looked upon the trip as a belated honeymoon. We had never taken an official one, because Jake was almost eight months pregnant by the time we finally got married. The trip was going to be loads of fun. We'd get through this and be back in showbiz by next pilot season. At least, that's what I told her. What I really had in mind was jumping out of the plane over Iceland.

As we passed a bored customs agent in Zürich, we weren't sure what to expect. Jakie was a little wrung out from the long flight, the lingering effects of the chemo, and the pain she was beginning to experience. I was by her side, scared to death, but giving her every ounce of support I could muster.

Our first meeting with Dr. Rau, the head of the clinic, went well. He was a warm, bearded man with a Swiss accent who, after checking her chart, welcomed us with, "So you're hoping for a miracle?" Jakie didn't react. It was almost as if she didn't hear him. I flinched and wondered what in heaven's name we were doing here.

Conversation Number Four

Earth is a learning ground, a laboratory. We are all part of the human experiment.

I'm mopey, whiney, feeling sorry for myself, and then I yawn, which means one of two things: Either I am exhausted and depressed, or my long-distance, out-of-town lover is coming to pay a visit. It turns out both possibilities are accurate. I'm feeling like crap and at the same time the hairs on my arms start to prickle, another sign that Jake is present.

"Hi, honey."

I hear her voice inside my head and hit the record button. "How are you?" I whine.

"I'm deliriously happy."

"Why did you have to go?" I kvetch.

"So much work, so little time."

"No, really, tell me."

"God called."

"I wish you stayed and got healthy and lived life with me."

"When God calls, you go." Jake had a great work ethic and attacked every job with gusto. When God offered the possibility of a new career, of course she said, "Here I am, Lord, where do you want me?"

"I'm so sad. I should be glad that I can still talk to you, but…why am I so sad?"

"Brokenhearted human love," she replies neutrally. I can sense her changing a little. She's a little less Jakie, more neutral, like a voice from far away, otherworldly, with less personality.

"I hurt so much." I start to snivel and weep. I guess the initial shock and numbness is wearing off and my grief is kicking in full bore.

"Of course you do. You had total devoted one hundred percent human love. Now it's time to move to higher love."

"How?" I plead. "Tell me how. And what the hell is higher love?"

"It's acceptance, cooperation, enthusiasm. Breathe in and out and cry the tears when they come. That's all you have to do, Michael; your destiny is programmed. Most everything that comes forward for you from now on—almost everything—will be from the fingertip of God. I would check everything out, of course, but I recommend you move forward on what comes to you. And know there is great support for your development."

That wasn't exactly the answer I had hoped for. It was a little general and didn't support my weakness enough. I wanted a concrete way to stop feeling so miserable. But her answer helped me converge and align my inner self. I forced myself to quit bitching, shaped up a tad, and decided to use our time together more productively. So I got all interviewy and asked, "What's it like 'crossing over'?" I deliberately chose a New Age phrase to impress her. After all, this was only our third date since she died.

"Wonderful," she responded delightfully.

"Oh, honey, I'm in agony. Will I ever see you again?" So much for keeping it positive. There I am, in the pits again.

"Yes, soul to soul. It will be different."

"Was dying hard?"

"No. Actually, it was kind of familiar. We've all been on this pathway many, many times before. Actually, it's quite familiar once you're out of the body."

"Do you still love me?" It's always about me, isn't it? Hey, I'm no different from anyone who has an ego, emotions, and a mind.

"Yes, in a bigger way."

"Do you miss the kids?"

"Not really; I'm with them."

"Any word for them?"

"Go team!"

"At Bobby's hoops, they broke the huddle with, '1–2–3 Jakie!' Bobby went for sixteen points and four assists."

"I don't care. You like basketball too much."

Wait, wait! I can't believe I heard those words. Jake loved hoops more than anyone in the world and had the sweetest, softest little jump shot, modeled after Jamal Wilkes' twenty-foot layup. Wow, things really are different. I was about to start arguing with her, but I didn't want her to leave, so I decided to schmooze her instead.

"Hey, beautiful, so uh, how do you communicate with other spirit people?" I casually flirted.

"Sensory knowing."

Great, now I know. Huh? "Are you still afraid of flying?"

"Nope."

Hmm, that's odd. Jakie always hated getting on a plane without the aid of a margarita or two. "What's the story on karma and soul progression?"

"Karma binds. It's not very important, only on earth. It just sets up lessons and growth. It gives personalities, like how much fun we had being indebted to each other."

"I'm a mess without you."

"You are a Light warrior, Michael, working to become pure Spirit. You chose a very difficult life pattern and said, 'Sock it to me.' Anyone lesser would be humbled. Go forward. Breathe the Light. Listen to the sound. You are growing in the Light and we will play again in higher realms."

"Can you tell me what it's like to die?"

"Sure. On that side you saw it. My soul was out of my body right after the boys left the hospital. My basic self was still running the physical body, breathing in and breathing out, even after the soul left. You travel thru the tunnel, thru the canal, up, very aware, into the Oneness where they read your records. Then, after the soul is transmuted into Light, there's a grand entrance into the arena of perfectly loving souls and above. It's very sacred. The adoring, amorous, melodic, engaging, tender feeling that exists there is magnificence. I was met by joyous beings and I knew I was home, in the supreme state of God's love and truth. This will be your next home. Your life will be a blessing. I have laid down energy fields that no one can destroy. Good shall prevail."

"Wow." I am speechless. That's magnificent, splendid, superb. A second of silence. Two seconds. Three. Four.

"Since I've been here," Jake, who's never at a loss for words, continues, "they've been teaching me ways to have contact with the physical plane and I've been helping people. I want to talk about what's expected of you. Listen carefully. You're to finish this grieving process quickly and you're to spend two hours a day with a pen in your hand, writing."

Whoa, my second directive. "Why?"

"So you become successful and prevail over the forces that hold you back."

This is too much to compute—too much information. Overload. Overload. I've got to slow down. I've got so many questions. Where do I start? Finally, I ask, "What about your clothes and stuff?" My god, what a stupid question.

"The criterion to guide you is whatever makes it easier. Don't dwell on any possession or anything. Ultimately, we don't take anything but our love with us. Save what you want to pass on to the kids."

"The kids have your rings."

"Fine."

"So practicality is the word?"

"Sell the house—whatever is best for you."

Another ohmigod! Sell the house? She would never have said anything like that when she was alive. She loved the house. Never. It was hugely symbolic. As I attempt to comprehend the enormity of it all, she continues, "The void of loneliness will soon be filled. You'll have some projects to work on to use your energy, your time. Tell the world about life after death. Right now, I invite you to be filled with joy and laughter and fun."

Sounds good to me. "Tell me about heaven," I say, now that I know everything is fine.

"From where I am, I can name the sinister forces affecting you and keep them away—the forces that hurt us while I was there. They are very picayune and easy to handle from this level. The planet itself is in a challenging place, but the spiritual war is really on a one-to-one basis. Protecting you is very important, because you're a convert to good, at least through your genetics. What you did to convert to the Light was challenging and we will keep you there. There's no need to save planets. It's in and for individual souls that the battle is being waged. We were dancing and glowing today. I'm a young spirit and they allow me a lot of leeway to have fun."

"Could you have been healed?"

"Yes, I could have been healthy. But God asked my high self to come."

"Was the timing perfect?"

"The timing was perfect."

"People love you so much, Jakie. What can I tell them?"

"Tell them I am fine, Michael, and that I love them back."

"I want to have some fun, Jakie. How do I do that?"

"You will. Get through the next few weeks; you're going to be fine. You got the message. The message is, 'Get over it! Get to work!' I'm alive. Love me. You can love me and another woman at the same time. She can love me. I'll send you one soon. If you want to get laid a little, go and do it. Just relax. Drinking is fine." My God, she's a party animal angel.

"Is there anything specific you can tell me so I know this isn't in my head?"

"The Lord Jesus Christ welcomes you into Christendom. The burdens you were given to bear this lifetime are being lifted from you. You are perfected and loved and appreciated for your hard work for the cause of good. Give Jesus your cross. Give him your burdens."

I will. I am. I start to yawn. An extraordinarily peaceful energy fills me, holds me, and caresses me. I am expanded and whole.

"God is soooo...*big*," Jakie says and starts to laugh uproariously. It's booming. She's having so much fun. "God is," she continues laughing. "You are. I am. You will be." Suddenly, the light, peaceful energy amps up, enveloping me. I almost feel like I'm floating.

"What are you doing?" I asked.

"I'm filling you with Light—taking more of your cares."

"I love you." I felt so close to her, as if nothing had changed, except she wasn't sick anymore. Jakie was lively and energetic and beautiful again. I continued, "We were really blessed, weren't we Jakie dear?"

"Yeah." And then, more magic. She kisses me through time and space. Smack on the lips. Whoa. An angel kiss. I swear, it felt so real. It was a loving peck, not a French kiss, but still...I was lying down when it happened and shot straight up. I raised my hand and felt my lips. Nope, nothing there. Damn, she's still a flirt.

"I just got an angel kiss. At least I think I did. It was so tempting, like a sexy flashbulb of electricity. Am I a crackpot?"

"Always have been, Michael, and so was I. We were made for each other. Now be still. I'm blessing you here. I'm protecting you. The same for Eli, Joey, Bobby, and David. That's it."

She was gone, but the sweet, blissful energy continued to caress me. Who needs a girlfriend, when I've got this?

Switzerland

No one goes through the world without being challenged. Challenges show where there is growth to be experienced. They reveal strengths waiting to come forward.

I feel like a blind man being pelted with rocks. I don't know who the enemy is, but he's out there. Thwack, the colon. Thud, the liver metastasizes. Ka-boom, ka-pow, a brick to the lymph system, gravel to the lungs. Well, the chemo didn't catch fire in the States, so here we are choosing the alternative route in Switzerland. The philosophy here is that people heal by strengthening their healthy parts and one of the clever ways to do this is by yanking unhealthy teeth. That's why I'm waiting for the dentist to extract the first of Jake's eight root canals. Eight—count them—eight. The prevailing thought in this one-horse burg is that root canals are linked to specific energetic meridians that can be the cause of great disease. I guess I was brainwashed into getting my root canals pulled, too. What do I know?

We started the day with a light breakfast at the Hotel Santis, an American-style motel inhabited by visitors to the clinic and their myriad of maladies. Shortly thereafter, a van arrives to pick us up for the trip to the clinic. It's several miles and Jakie's not strong enough to walk it. Besides, it's pretty chilly, it being almost springtime in the Alps and all.

At the clinic, Jakie goes from far-out treatment to really far-out treatment, many of them illegal in the States. In a funny way, it's like being in college together, walking from class to class. We kiss goodbye and she does her thing, which is to get better, and I do mine, which is to hang out. I mostly sit and think as I wait for the verdict to be read. Is it life or death for my loved one, my most cherished, the one who brought me alive, the one who knows my thoughts before I think them, whose eyes sparkle when she laughs, who kicks me under the table to shut up? My angel. The one who returned me back to my goodness, back to my caring, my conduit to God. Damn! You can't imagine the emptiness I feel without her. And she's still here.

I peek in and see my sweetie-pie, small and sweet in the dental chair. My heart goes out to her, poor baby. I return to my seat and nervously thumb through a pile of Swiss magazines. Man, are they dull! Martina Hingis with her clothes on. Who cares?

So here I am in the town of Lustmühle, next to the town of Teufen, outside St. Gallen, outside Zürich, outside the United States, checking out the women in the dental office. The Swiss chicks aren't really my type—a little too big in the tush, a lot too small on top. I prefer it the other way. God, do you believe me? I mean, how shallow can I be? Here I am, feeling thoroughly frightened and abandoned, having to consider the possibility that the best thing that ever happened in my whole, entire life may be taken away and look at what I'm doing. I'm leering. I'm a sophomoric, horny jerk, but whoa, that one's kind of hot. My mind, I've got to stop my mind, and I've got to stop being so hyper and stop judging myself and—

Wow, it's really too bad that I hadn't had the cosmic conversations with Jakie yet. I'm sure if I did, I'd have been easier on myself. I'd have been more relaxed with the knowledge that her dying was on purpose—that no one leaves here unless the soul gives the okay. Nor did I have the slightest clue as to how much I would grow spiritually.

We stayed at the clinic for five weeks. Jakie was pretty strong when we arrived, and we started out on a somewhat hopeful note. In the beginning, we'd go for little walks in the crisp, cold air. I'd adorn her in a six-foot scarf, she'd hold one end, and I'd run around her until she was wrapped up tight. I'd make her a snowball to throw, grab her hand, and off we'd go.

We explored the town, all four blocks of it. We discovered the computer at the local library where we checked out March Madness basketball scores. We visited local restaurants, where only nominal tipping—a few little coins—is expected. We window-shopped the stores on the main drag, a bunch of bakeries and butcher shops with pig's heads and sausages proudly displayed.

Our tenure in Teufen was a transitional time for Jakie, and while we were there our relationship began to shift. Jakie slowly started turning inward, moving away from me, and there was nothing I could do about it. Ultimately, our closeness stopped short of me being able to breathe her breath for her. No matter how much I love her, I'm still not inside. I came to realize that when you're facing death, you have to face it alone. But are we ever really alone? Could there be a higher power going through everything with us? I hope so. I believe when we are facing our final days, we are alone with God.

I look over at her, and she has a sly smile on her face. I wonder if she's accepting her fate. I wonder if there's a spiritual part that knows. I'm so afraid of losing her. The love she beams to others is the love she beams to me. She put up with so much—my tirades, my anger—and she's always hung in. She lifted me to where I am now. Whoa, check out the babe who just walked in. Now that is fine. There I go again. Michael, stop it!

The mind of a man in my position is not a pretty sight. I'm trying to be a good guy. I'm here for Jake, I really am. I'm busy trying to figure out what causes cancer so I can save her. My latest theory is that it's a combination of genetics, environment, nutrition, and the negative aspects of our personality coming back to kill us. All that, coupled with a plethora of demonic spirits that we earned by leading less than exemplary lives during the sum total of all our past incarnations. Sure, those devilish little critters are invisible, but that doesn't mean they don't influence us.

I wasn't brought up believing in reincarnation and past lives, but living in the cancer world of life and death certainly raises the question. Maybe the content of our present existence was set up a long, long time ago? Maybe it's true: One lifetime we're up, king of the world, a James Cameron, living large. And then, next lifetime, payback—the Titanic sinks. Eastern religions call this phenomenon karma, where all our past actions are returned to us. *Karma.* It's a silly '60s word that makes my ancestors uncomfortable. Karma is simple: "What you sow, so shall ye shall reap." "Ye?" Okay, let's try, "What goes around, comes around," or as the childhood Brooklyn street ditty goes, "I'm rubber and you're glue, whatever you say bounces off me and sticks to you."

Basically, karma means, if you dance, you've got to pay the band. God knows it pays to be nice, because God knows. Maybe there are records of all our actions and if we die owing a debt—like for cheating, lying, killing, or being self-destructive—then, *bam,* God socks it to us in our next life. That's the law: payback for all our past negativity—physical, emotional, mental, and unconscious—coupled with the genetics of our ancestors. Down to the last dime.

And there's only one way out of this seemingly hopeless pattern: God's grace. That's what I am counting on, the miracle of lifting above the Law. Grace is when the Big Guy, El Señor, wipes the slate clean. Hey, why not? He can; he's God, for godsakes. He can do whatever the hell he wants.

Jakie suddenly appears, interrupting my endless, pulsating mind chatter, and shoots me a sheepish grin. We laugh and I hug her. There's nothing but empty space where two of her fetching upper teeth used to hang. She leans in and surrenders. I hold her tightly; she has that funny dental odor.

"Tell me a story," she says sweetly, "one with a happy ending."

"Okay, I'm going to enlighten and entertain you with a love story about God extending grace to two loony young lovers. She, a living angel with stage four cancer. He, a lonely shell of a man, horribly out of place in a country where everyone pays retail." She laughs; I can still make her laugh. Thank heavens.

As we head out to our next class, I ponder, *Damn, I hope my view of grace is correct, because if it is, we have a chance. Otherwise, it's over for her and the hell of loneliness for me.* God, we need a miracle.

Conversation Number Five

Higher consciousness means loving the Creator and loving the creation. All of it.

Saturday, May 27. Jakie's been gone from her home on earth for nine days. I'm puttering around the house, gloomy and down, when out of the blue, prickles and a yawn. I get the chills and the hairs on my arms come erect.

"I'm yawning, honey. Hi." I feel Jakie's presence and start to snivel and moan like a sad little boy. I run into the bedroom, grab the tape recorder, and start yapping away.

"I took care of you so long and so hard," I tell her, wiping my nose.

"Those tears have to come, Michael. Those tears have to come." Suddenly, I feel the soothing hand of Spirit on my shoulder, as she gently informs me, "You loved at a very high rate and it hasn't gone unnoticed in heaven."

"Thank you. Tell me more about what happens in Spirit. Is it great from the first second you leave the body?"

"Yes. You lift to the vibration of your loving, to the highest level of Spirit the soul can maintain. Now, relax, I want to tell you about a beautiful place I saw yesterday. There was an elegant, shimmering, somewhat crystal, vapor lake, but not really like that. You lie there and vibrations move through your consciousness. Through loving, all ties and all pulls and all vibrations of your past life are eradicated, lifted. That's why people on earth sometimes feel so liberated when a loved one dies. I did that yesterday, so everyone will be freer. You were taken there in the dream state, and Eli, Joey, and Bobby were all taken there to release their ties to me. The ties you have now will be mental and memories. We will no longer be able to pull each other's chain.

"Loving and togetherness are automatic for souls that vibrate so closely, like ours. We will be reunited in a soul-realm mansion. Spirit is working closely with our family. I'm glad you broke the bonds of your hurt little inner child looking for strings attached to all the gifts that are being offered to you. Now you can accept the charity in the sweetness that it is offered. I've been working with a lot of our friends and family. In terms of the people you don't like coming to the memorial, please allow them the opportunity to forgive themselves. Don't restrict anything or anyone; be as kind as you can. Your burdens have been lifted. Allow that ease for others. Take care of yourself physically. Start walking more."

One, two, three, four, five. It takes a long time for all that information to sink in. Six, seven, eight, nine— Finally, I respond, "Do you sleep?" Damn, I'm such an idiot; is that the best I can come up with? Unbelievable! If this were a first date, she'd dump me.

"No," Jake answers patiently. "We're in a constant state of awareness and beauty." She pauses for a beat, then, "And you know the story of us, chasing each other through many lifetimes, coming to earth together and falling in love many, many times is highly accurate. Truly, I have been loving you forever. The completion is beautiful."

"Honey-pie, what's the best way for me to get through this?"

"Walk and breathe and write and clean house and get out when you can. Now, just bask in the energy of fulfillment and loving. Here's the Inner Master. He's going to join us." Slowly, like a calming fog rolling in, the room begins to fill with a blissful energy.

"Lighten up," she goes on. "God loves you and God is with you. You are a man, and in my earth body, I loved you with all my heart, as you loved me." I start to cry as tears burst forth from the depth of my deepest love. My body wails and rocks and shudders until I feel that comforting invisible hand on my shoulder again.

"There's something else I want you to be aware of. I was in a place—it was purple, with orange headlights and hanging lights. Anyway, it feels like that. It's an energy field that's calming, trusting, and that's being placed with you and Joey right now. We're adding in the missing pieces, adding on greater strength and power. You'll feel the same, but you'll have access to this and you'll be perceived in a greater way." Wow, what a nice little gift. I start to yawn and stretch as my awareness of Spirit, as I imagine it, intensifies.

"I'm reinforcing your stomach, putting energy around it so you can't be tipped over and fearful."

I yawn again. "Mmmmm, this feels so good." Then, my mood changes abruptly. "Ohhh Jakie, I keep seeing you all sick in my mind. You were so lively and alive." There I go again.

"I told you, I'm even more vibrant now, Mike. More than you can imagine. I was always held back by my karma, my choices, my health and now, I'm free and exploding. I am more the way you always pictured me. Sometimes, you saw my magnitude more than I did and wondered why I held myself back. Well, I don't anymore. Not in the least. I am shooting stars and radiant nights and fireworks and explosives and hydrogen bombs and laughter and joy and meaning and clarity and caring and joyousness and triumphant music and exploding firecrackers and roman candles and peace and quiet and noise and orchestras and tympani drums and choirs and shouting and loving. No soul can be contained. I'm so grateful to be free."

"Do you have recollection of your life?

"Vaguely, from this place I do. As soon as I leave, I don't. I'm getting a little dispensation here to work with people because of our partnership and your growth into the Light."

"What happens when you leave and move to heaven; we won't be talking anymore?" I'm a little scared.

"Don't worry. I can be reached through the heart. I'll always be there."

Suddenly, I started to feel so woozy I had to lie down. I felt like I had the weight of a heavy comforter all over me, I checked and nothing was there. Through a huge yawn I managed to ask, "Are you doing me?"

"No, it's being done thru the masters of the colors, through stepping down energetic matrixes of the 93rd order, angels, vibratory frequencies, metamorphosing, and delineation matrixes."

"Huh?'

"It's like electricity; you don't have to know how it works. All you need to do is turn on the switch."

"Am I going to be different?" I was starting to get a little nervous from the unusual feeling, even though I knew Jakie would never hurt me.

"Not at first; it's a gradual thing. Like a dimmer going up, outside your body, white hot heat that isn't hot. You're coming alive. I'm going to keep filling you up. Top off your tank, so to speak."

I started sobbing, I felt so loved and cared for. "I'm crying, thinking about what an angel you are."

"Yes I am. More than you can imagine. I am expanding and expanding and expanding and expanding. It's like everything I told you yesterday is a lie; it's all quantumly larger now. It's monumental and astounding and brilliant."

"What do you do all the time?"

"God's will," she said simply. "Right now, that means helping you." Wow, God has me on his radar.

"You're being reprogrammed, downloaded. We're loading in the ability for you to be quiet; that's a new one for you." And she laughs. No one ever knew me like she did, uh, I mean, does.

"There is a place in heaven with the holograms of willow trees. It's an oasis of sorts. Peace is being added to you."

"Good, I feel like a character in *The Matrix*."

"Relax, everything is fine. Creativity is being enhanced. It comes from a light show—kind of strobing, but not really."

Suddenly, the phone rings and I am pulled out of my reverie. "I don't want to get it. This is too peaceful." I let it ring; there's no one on this planet I'd rather be talking to right now. Or off this planet, either.

"Tell me everything. Tell me more about heaven and what happens when we die."

"My job is to support you, not pass along all the secrets of Spirit. I'm lining up things, so your life will roll gently downhill."

"Awwwww, it feels so good."

"They're putting in ease and relaxation."

"What's that dark thing I see?"

"It's like a funnel—a vortex going into you—offering greater ease and peace."

"How about helping me become a deeper breather?"

"Sorry, that's a habit; you have to consciously work on that."

"Honey, tell me something I don't know."

"That's not my job," she said.

I continued to work on her. I have my ways. We could always get a secret out of each other, even if we promised not to tell. "Come on. I'll be your best friend. Just one thing, please, please."

"Oh-kay." Yes, I've still got it. "There's a church in heaven with the most beautiful bells that are not really bells, which ring with an inner vibration."

"Is it the sound current?" The sound current is mentioned in many religions and disciplines. It has been described as the audible stream of energy that comes from the heart of God. In the Christian Bible, it is referred to as "the Word." There is a yoga tradition that focuses on the sound current called Shabda Yoga.

"It's the source of the sound current."

Then I lost it and started crying again, not because of what she said, but because of how sad I started feeling. "Oh Jakie, I wish you were here. It's so lonely. I miss you—your smell, your hair, your smelly hair." I start to laugh and cry.

"You can't have that, but you can love me."

"I'm having a weepy day. Am I crying for you or me?"

"A little bit of both. Your sadness is crying for me. When that's gone, your heart will cry and laugh and love and illuminate. That's what we're working toward. You're giving up your burdens. And give the people my message. Tell them to laugh and love and live, to be happy and know that you don't die. Call it, *A Message from Jakie*. And have little quotes from Spirit at the top of each chapter."

"Okay, okay." Then I had a really great thought and I started to laugh. I told her, "I may rewrite it. I have the last pass now." I pictured her smiling in Spirit and asked, "Are you really happy?"

"Happy doesn't describe it, Michael. Happy is an earth term. It's emitting colors; it's power; it's projection; it's waterfalls, reindeer, rain dances, music, bells, beauty; it's the sound current. God, it's loving; it's holding, caressing, kissing; and it's all waiting for you, Michael. As soon as you die, your path will be clear. Let me give you a kiss." *Wow! Wowee!* I pucker up. It's out of this world—extraordinary.

"And Michael," she persists, "remember, like Joey said, 'be grateful for the greatest life you could've had.'"

Wishing and Hoping

With grace there is an opportunity to move directly to where we are going.

After her teeth are pulled, the next stop on the healing parade at the Paracelsus Clinic is the bioresonance and magnetic field therapy room. Popular theory interprets this treatment as supportive in eliminating toxic materials such as mercury and palladium, relieving pain, calming the nerves by slightly depolarizing them, de-acidifying the treated area, and improving the magnetic potential of the tissue, which is a prerequisite for vitality.

Of course, it's only a short hop and a jump to assume that without the toxic metals and the negative pressure they bring to her invisible energetic meridians, Jakie's immune system will work better; her body will rise up and defeat the cancer. She'll become an old lady, get wrinkles, her boobs will sag, and we'll all live happily ever after. Until we die of something else, many, many years from now.

She's lying down, a little wrung out from her oral ordeal, when I start singing the Lovin' Spoonful's, *Do You Believe in Magic* to amuse her—and considering my voice, trust me, it's amusing. I was really getting into rhyming *groovy* with *movie*, when a pretty Swiss nurse enters and informs us that a temporary dental bridge will be ready for my cutie-pie in an hour, thanks to the in-house laboratory.

"Isn't that wonderful?" the nurse asks.

"No!" That's not soon enough for Jakie, who pleads, "Michael, you've got to hide me 'til it's ready."

"I will," I promise. "I'll chew your food if you want." As if I haven't been doing that for years? She smiles for a second, but quickly covers up, concealing the prominent space in her grill. I continue my serenade, "...if you believe in magic don't bother to choose—" But in spite of my illustrious vocals, the smile did wipe off, because Jakie was fully committed to not showing her teeth—or rather, revealing the lack of them. She's always been a touch vain. Who can blame her? The girl knows she's a hottie and doesn't relish looking any less than the delectable morsel she is. In fact, early in the cancer game, her biggest fear was that the chemo would make her hair fall out. And in her view, in spite of the grave situation she's in, having a stupid-looking smile is right up there with being bald. I wanted to get her mind off herself, so I quickly came up with a game. It's a technique we use on the kids. It's a little number we like to call "conscious manipulation." I piqued her interest by suggesting we pitch out the story of our lives as if we were presenting it for a TV series. That's what we do for a living and she sparked to it.

"Let's talk casting first. Who would you pick to play me?" she asked excitedly.

"That's easy, Jakie. Meg Ryan, but only in her prime. What about me?" I asked.

"It's always about you, isn't it, Michael?"

"Yes. C'mon, who should be me? And don't say Billy Crystal; they already did that movie."

Jakie scrunched up her face, thought about it for a long time, and then she went, "I know. Cary Grant. You're as handsome as he is any day and you've both got that sexy cleft chin." And you wonder why I love her so much.

"Good answer," I said, kissing her. "Now let's start developing the characters," I pressed on. "What are these people made of? What are they like? What kind of ice cream do they eat?" She groaned and I smiled knowingly. That's the kind of stupid question pompous producers always ask writers.

"I know I don't want to be like the characters in *Love Story*," she kind of whispered.

"Don't worry, honey, I could never be like Oliver Barrett. I'm poor, Jewish, and don't play hockey. The only thing we have in common is we both hate our fathers."

"Well, I don't want to be Ali MacGraw."

"Why not? She's beautiful."

"She's too tall. And besides—she died."

"Oh yeah, so as I was saying—" I chattered, adroitly changing the subject. "Let's talk about me."

"I know," Jakie mused, equally willing to move on, "we'll make your character really normal and ordinary—just your typical, average American."

"True, true, I am just like everyone else." That is, if everybody has forty-seven credit cards and owes over $140,000. Give or take a late payment. Really. I don't bother Jake with the details, but I am spending at least $3,500, or about 5,000 Swiss francs a week, to have these bizarre treatments continue. Not counting room and board. Who cares if I'm broke? I charge to the likes of Chase Manhattan, MBNA, Centurion, Wells Fargo, Wachovia, Discover, MasterCard, Visa, American Express, Green, Optima, Blue, Bank One, Sumitomo, Citibank, and on and on. I am an equal opportunity borrower. What do you want me to do? Let her die? So what if I am spending money I don't have on a belief I have to have? God will save my girl. God knows it won't be a doctor. "Doctor, doctor, give me the news, I've got a bad case of lovin' you."

"Let's make it a love story. I love love stories," the delightful woman speaks. Ain't that the truth? No matter how bad a movie is, she's happy at the end if she can go, "Oooo, they're kissing."

"But, honey, a compelling love story needs interesting, heroic characters and since I'm starring in this one, I'm not sure it qualifies."

"Oh, Michael!" she blurted out. Those are the two words I've probably heard the most in my life. *Oh, Michael.* She doesn't like it when I get down on myself, so I changed my tone.

"Okay, I know I project to the world okay. Clever, a little cocky, good-looking for a guy my age."

"And which age is that?" my dear one inquires. Oh, by the way, I have several ages. One, my real age, and the second, a variable age for my job in show business.

"Today, let's say I'm forty-five." I'm not. I'm older. I lie to continue working, because Hollywood is youth obsessed. Everyone is older than they say they are. Trust me, Jerry Lewis is not the forty-seven his bio swears him to be.

"Forty-five, hmmm? Well, maybe you could pass. You do have that hip look; you're lean if you don't count the belly. I like your five hundred dollar intellectual glasses and love your smug smile."

"It's all sheen, like a china vase on a decorative shelf; I look good, but I'm useless. My life would make a really piss-poor love story. Let's make it a comedy instead. Please?" I persist.

"C'mon, big boy, I love you. So it has to be a love story. A modern-day love story."

"Fine, honey, but what are love stories today? They're all about callow, shallow, horny characters. The classics had good-looking, tough, masculine guys well into their forties. C'mon, how old was Bogart in *Casablanca*?"

"You're right," she retorts. "Today, they'd ask him to play a grandpa in a sitcom."

"If he'd come in and read for the part?" A clever comeback, if I do say so myself.

"See, you're perfect for my love story, Michael. You're old enough to be a grandfather." That was a good one, too, and to drive the point home, she smiled wide for the first time, forcing me to notice where her recently evacuated choppers used to exist.

"Stop that. You're turning me on," I laughed.

"Enough about you; it's my turn. I'm the female star—the heroine—and I've got to be unique by Hollywood standards."

"That you are, my pet."

"I know. How many leading ladies are cancer victims with tons of missing teeth?"

"You got me there." I smile, but inside what I am really thinking is, *Who is the victim here? My wife, who is faced with a seemingly hopeless situation, or the inadequate husband who can't do a damn thing to help her?*

"Let's call Spielberg," I suggest, hiding my pain. "How can he resist the love story of a powerless man in love with a woman who shits in a bag?" Time's up. The nurse comes in.

It was fun verbally sparring with Jakie. We used to go at it all the time, and even if she isn't quite up to her old standards, she's still adorable to me. What a trooper. It's amazing she still has her sense of humor.

After the day's treatments, we go back to our hotel room to read and rest. It's a quiet time when I can nurture her and tend to her needs. I make sure she takes her pills and I give her an injection of Iscador, a mistletoe concoction they say helps. I fill a hypodermic needle with the medicine, tap out any air bubbles, pinch her belly, and let it fly. Amazingly, it barely hurts. Today, I hold the ampoule over her head like it's a sprig of mistletoe at Christmas and try to kiss her. She's too pooped to buy my charm.

About the only thing I look forward to is talking to the kids on the phone. Just hearing their voices lifts me, but we have to time it. Add seven hours, but reverse the time of day, or something like that. Basically, if we call early in the morning, we get them at night. It's so nice to hear the minutia of their lives—school, friends, and the parties. It makes me cry how much I love them and then I consider what those poor, sweet guys have in store for them just around the corner.

Lots of times, Jake's so fatigued she falls asleep on my shoulder. She doesn't talk much most of the time, and usually by this time of day, she says even less. It gives me more time to ruminate. Oh joy! I wonder what's going on inside Jake's mind. What does she know, what does she expect, what is she feeling? Is she scared? She sure doesn't act like it. Oh man, she's put up with so much, fighting like hell to get better. Damn, she's only forty-six. It's not fair. She hasn't even had her midlife crisis. I'm sure she feels gypped—she's got these kids and me and all the pulls of her life.

Even with her sweet face on my shoulder, I feel more alone than I've been for a long time. My biggest fear is returning to my old thoughtless and narcissistic ways if she doesn't stick around. It was so right and I was so married when we met. I was in love for the first time, I hoped it was gonna last, it felt like a love that could last forever, like a love that has no past. Please, Jakie, don't let me down, not after all I've gone through, all the guilt and trauma and confronting of my childhood conditioning that I had to release for us to be together. Not after we've been so happy, sleeping so closely together, sucking in each other's air and living to tell the tale. The drinking, the hot sex. Even the fights. Who cares about the slammed doors, the flung dishes, or the curse words? I love being with you, maturing with you, growing up with you alongside our kids. I love all the wonderful events and milestones in our loving and blessed life: the birth of our babies, watching their first rides on a two-wheeler, the trip to Dodger Stadium when they freaked out at the fireworks, David's soccer games, Eli teaching himself words like Cincinnati and Boston so he could read the sports page, his winning touchdown in seventh grade, Joey's playfully hiding in a dresser drawer when he was three, his graffiti days, and Bobby hopping across the room sideways in his rubber ducky jockey shorts, cracking us up with his exuberance.

The weekends here are pure misery. There is nothing to do except obsess, get on each other's nerves, and be aware of the pain. Did you ever notice that pain goes away when you're focused on other things? But there is nothing to do.

If I only had a hint of the beautiful celestial realm she was about to move to, I might have been able to distract myself with enchanted thoughts about the arena of perfectly loving souls and the melodic magnificence that exists there. Too bad.

My Honeymoon

Watch out for rules. Like, the captain always goes down with the ship. Why? What if there's room in the lifeboat? But that's the rule! Then that's a stupid rule.

As Jake continues to get her treatments, I sit and wait wearily, with my private thoughts. It's one of the ways the partner of a cancer-impaired woman amuses himself on his "honeymoon." I am lost in my mind and emotions, even as she appears to have risen above hers. Nothing fazes her. What amazes me is how Jakie floats through the day with a light, airy smile, with never a cross word or moment of frustration as she is subjected to the endless cure. She has sweetness for all the doctors and nurses and love, warmth, and concern for the other patients. Her focus is simply on the next thing presented. My focus is on my own petty thoughts and what will happen to me if she dies.

Up to this point, I have pretty much deluded myself into seeing her healthy, but lately, icky sticky pictures have been popping into my mind. Like, late one night real early in the process, a frightened Jakie wanted me to ask the fledgling doctor on call a question. The annoyed medicine man couldn't have been nastier. His attitude was like, "Why are you bothering me? She has stage four cancer, for Christsakes." I remember my tummy falling and swallowing his harsh words, smiling at Jakie, and making up an answer to protect her. It's funny—every time I saw that guy after that I got pissed off, while Jakie just beamed him love.

We saw Dr. Rau today and he said cancer couldn't be fought; it must be loved and changed with tenderness. Screw him. Love and tenderness? The whole world is dense. People are constantly looking for trouble—starting fights, flipping each other off. Road rage is the norm. We need our hourly squirt of adrenalin. That's how I relate. Hate, anger, and revenge drove me—drove me nuts during my teen and college years. As a young man in my twenties, I was angry and shallow, drinking too much, smoking this and that, numbing my pain, and raging at others. Why did she even love me? There's only one purely logical explanation I can come up with. Our love affair was destined and she didn't have a choice.

Living is hard. There are so many ways to feel inferior, ineffectual, and unworthy. Like at night, lying side-by-side with my most cherished and not being able to do a damn thing to help her. It really, really sucks. She saved my life. She made me a better person, a good man. Not an easy task, considering where I started. The least I can do is return the favor. I was well into my thirties when we met. Who still has hope at that age? I didn't, but she tricked me. She was too wonderful, too great a dresser, too sexy, too smart, too awesome. I fell for real and for good. And that's what supplied the missing ingredient in my life. True love. That's what we gave to each other, true love, true love." "Love Me Tender." "All You Need is Love." "Love is a Many Splendored Thing." Suddenly, all the songs had meaning. I would die for Jake. Do you want to know a secret? If you promise not to tell? Whoa oh, oh. I am now about to my reveal my secret for happiness on this planet. Being loved is important, but the real key is *loving someone else*. When we met, I finally got to give love, wholly, holy, completely, fully, with every cell of my being. The dam had burst. And then I showered my cascading torrent of love onto the children she gave me, with the same enormous power. God bless you, Jakie.

And do you want to know the tricky part? Through the years, bitter and hurt little Mikey slowly transformed into a good guy—an honest, loyal, generous, and caring man. I grew up. I'm nice now, no longer controlled by my father's rage or my own, and I give all the credit to Jake and my love for her. Please, God, let her stick around so I can keep on healing myself.

Meanwhile, Back in Teufen

You've done all you could; there is no more to do. When you're so exhausted you can't lift a finger, life is telling you this is coming to a close. Get ready for some downtime.

The saga continues. My woman, as the Germans call their wives, is on a mission to reverse the cancer. Her human side wants to live and remain among her loved ones. Her human side wants the suffering to stop. She's put up with so much pricking and poking. I imagine she's praying, "Lord, take this burden from me. Let me be with my family. Let me be with my children. Let me be with my lover." She's doing everything in her power to fight it. Why else would she consent to having more teeth pulled?

After that ordeal, her dentist slips me a baggy with her pulled teeth in it and reminds me to hold onto it. Apparently, the energy of her extracted teeth is vital to the healing process. That's why I was absolutely beside myself when I realized I lost the baggy.

Man, I've been on a mission here, to be the perfect lover, caring nurse, supportive friend, and loyal advocate, and I've batted a thousand up 'til now. Keeping track of supplements and homeopathic remedies, giving injections no matter how much shots give me the willies, cheerleading, getting her back and forth to the clinic, feeding her, loving her, telling jokes—doing whatever it takes—and *I lost the baggy*.

It was my first and only slipup, but inside of me, I consider it a major blunder. *I lost the teeth*, and for want of a tooth, an army shall die. She asked me to do one lousy thing and I couldn't pull it off. There I am, bummed out, beating myself up, rushing around the clinic, tears in my eyes, bumping into morphined-out cancer patients with IV infusions, looking for teeth in all the wrong places. As I dart about, Dr. Rau stops me and says, "Your wife—she wants heat, full body? There is a cancellation." Shit, yeah.

The scuttlebutt among the victims—er, patients—is that systemic hyperthermia is the deepest, most powerful therapy they offer here. So we cancel Jake's other appointments and get her over to a reflective, silvery thermal box, get her zipped up in this aluminum foil space-suit-type thingy, and start heating her up. It makes a little sense. Fevers have long been recognized to be one of the body's natural ways of healing itself, and this treatment deliberately creates one. Again, so simple.

They start her up. We want to get as high as possible—104 or 105 degrees—to burn the son of a bitch out. We learn that the process works on more than the physical level. It somehow drives the body back to a primal state. Fantasies, thoughts, and feelings emerge, scorched out from hidden caves buried deep within the unconscious. It roots out hidden emotional and mental energy, strong enough to grow a cancer, strong enough to create a death wish, and strong enough to silently kill.

Jakie's treatment was miraculous. She regressed in years and proceeded to express in a way she was never allowed to as a child. She cried and bawled and blubbered and sobbed. She realized, on a deep, deep level, how her father dismissed her, the fear she felt when her old man turned a rifle on her mother when Jake was still in the crib, and much, much, more that was hurtful and wounding. A torrent of memories came pouring out: her mom's battle with diet pills, an insane and nasty grandma who pushed mom into a failed attempt at becoming a child star, an opium-addicted grandpa who gave Jakie a nickel to brush his greasy hair. The drunken parties she witnessed with passed-out adults strewn around the pool after raucous nights of calling each other "Clyde" and acting like Sinatra's Rat Pack. Ring a ding ding. A little girl wandering around a house where no one was ever really sure who was sleeping with who. At one soiree, one of her mom's tipsy girlfriends hit on Jakie and tried to lock her in the bedroom. Jakie grew up in a world where the kids were programmed to tell mom—Darlene—what a great ass she had.

Thoughts popped out about a dog she loved as a child and their mildly erotic relationship. Tears flowed over the lonely days she spent as her family's indentured servant, not being allowed to go out and play until the house was clean. There was the shame of her parents' lifestyle and divorce in the straightlaced 1950s. And all the boozing— the excessive boozing—where the good life was defined as an Old Fashioned glass brimming with scotch. One cube, please. There was the pain of watching the big brothers she loved so dearly being soundly punished by her uptight and authoritarian stepfather. Tears of rage and shame erupted about being taken out back to be whipped and having to cut her own switch for the dirty deed. Melancholy about getting accepted at Stanford University and not being able to go because no one cared. Toss in her mom's pride in teaching her only daughter the fine art of shoplifting, minor indignities like her brother's friends peeking in her window, and freaking out on acid at a Doors concert and having to maintain when she got home. Not to mention the huge void of the family's lack of connection. It was extraordinary. This treatment assisted in the unearthing of her deepest, darkest, most hidden secrets, and after a rather intense time and many, many tears, we hoped they were history.

Back in our hotel room, I lovingly and gently tuck my baby into bed and she quickly falls into a deep, cathartic sleep.

I gaze out the window and see some kids shooting baskets at the sports center down below and ponder, *Boy, those Swiss kids sure suck at hoops.* Also, *Europeans appear much more accepting of death. Maybe Americans are, too, and I just live in L.A.*

I have too much time to think.

Dreams

You are being given an opportunity to look at yourself as you turn a corner. To rise to the level of how you do life, so it gets more clear and bright.

Today was a really bad day. We got the results of several recent cancer marker blood tests. CEA-62. Something else, 200 plus. These numbers are too high. It says the cancer is active. Luckily, I was able to distract myself by watching the largest snowflakes I've ever seen in my life. They were dumping from the sky, silently and peacefully. For a second, I was happy and calm, drifting with the snowflakes as they melted on the wet pavement and disappeared. When I was a kid, the prevailing mythology was that no two snowflakes were alike. Today, I doubt that very much. Out of all the snow that has fallen since forever, there've had to have been at least two that were identical. And for those of you who believe that "for every drop of rain that falls, a flower grows," I say, BS. No way! If that were true there would be no room for people. The world would be a jungle of tulips, daffodils, and lilies of the valley. See how we're programmed? I'm positive I'm not the only gullible doofus who's bought into the snowflake scam, but it makes you wonder. How many more of our most sacred beliefs are bogus?

"I'd like to think this experience has made us better people." Those were the words that Jake spoke in a moment of lightness. Damn, she's a trooper and her eyes can still sparkle. She is awesome, cracking jokes in the midst of it all. I am one lucky dude.

That night, I have an extremely disconcerting dream. I start out watching tennis on TV next to a healthy and young Jakie. It's the U.S. Open, a sure sign that school is about to begin. Suddenly, we're playing against each other and she's blasting fireballs at me. I am ducking and cowering before her power. She wins easily, running me from side to side until I am exhausted. After the final point, she approaches the net, gives me a perfunctory kiss, raises her arms to the adoring crowd, and explodes into flames.

As I trudge off the court, I look back and see myself interviewing the victor. Holding a microphone up to a ball of flame I ask, "Honey, I've been curious. I've always wondered what you thought when you first got the news, about being sick and all."

"Oh Michael, I was so scared," she says. "But I was rejoicing at the same time."

"Huh? Why?"

"I knew the outcome all along, I knew it before I was born, but I was conflicted. I didn't want to let you guys down. I'm doing the treatments for you and the kids."

"Are you praying for God to heal you?"

"Of course I am. Who wants to suffer?"

"Where are you in the process right now?"

"I'm torn—torn between the loss of everything I love here versus the bliss of being with God, with his beautiful colors and music soothing me, loving me, caressing me, lifting me."

Shit, I thought, *Doesn't seem like a very tough choice.*

"Trust me. It's not." She laughs. Man, I hate this dream so much, I force myself to get up and go to the bathroom to stop it.

In the morning, I wake up with a queasy, uneasy feeling. I look out the window and try to relax. It's a rainy, snowy day and I allow my gaze to soften. I hear an inner voice telling me to be like the beautiful lone tree, standing gracefully on the bucolic farmland slope. Since I don't hear inner voices very often—at least I didn't at that time— I listened and thought about what it would be like to be the tree. Sturdy, patient, oblivious to changes in the weather, hot or cold, snow, sleet, or rain. Standing there day after day, loyal, graceful, firm, beautiful, and steadfast. That's my perception, but to really be the tree, I must know its innermost thoughts and feelings. I have to have the experience of that living organism. All of a sudden I am filled with tree knowledge. In the center of that tree, at its core, it knows it will be nourished, in the right and proper order of nature. And day in and day out, it trusts that all its needs will be provided. And that's the space I'm told I need to move to—trusting I will be fed on all levels, trusting that all is right in the universe. I need to give up my fear and worry and anger so I can offer my loved one some shade, some comfort, some peace. And all the while—calmly and in a stately, elegant manner—I am aware I will be nourished. I will be taken care of; at this moment, I know this to be true.

That's the good news. The bad news is that my sweetheart is in excruciatingly intense pain and they can't give her heavy-duty morphine painkillers, because they'll block some of the treatments. Suddenly, there is a lot less laughter.

Later, there is more less-than-good news. Rather, let's call it "the other news." Like the tree that I am, I am staying neutral. It's probably easier on the tree, because the tree didn't just find out that his wife's swollen lymph nodes impinged on some nerves in her kidney.

It's weird, but Jake could live with all these little dots of cancer in her and be fine if they never grew, or, as in this case, did not affect nerves and cause her so much anguish that she wants to get out of here. And I mean the planet, not the clinic. The pain is so atrocious, I am afraid that she is willing to die to feel better.

I may be moving into stupid territory here, but I think Jake is at that place in her current incarnation—that's today, for you non–New-Age thinkers—where She, not the little she, but the total godlike big *She*, decides whether to live or die.

As a child, I had several unwritten rules. One, I'd cut my nose off to spite my face in order to win. Two, I could act more crazy, more violent, and more insane than anyone, to get them to back off. I thank Daddy for that little talent. Jakie's most famous rule to live by—the one embroidered into the sampler of her mind—was, "I'm losing, I quit." My fear is that this creed is still invisibly working within her, not burned out by the heat treatments.

Damn, I know she can be a fighter! She survived giving birth to three sons, a scornful ex-wife, showbiz, and my wonderful personality, and she's never given up. She has been battered, bloodied, and cut, yet she continues on. She's tougher than Nick Nolte, pumped full of lead, staggering down the railroad tracks in *Who'll Stop the Rain?* Does she have what it takes to keep on keeping on? I hope so. I don't have to be the hero; she does. I'm simply a stupid tree in a stupid country that doesn't even have its own language.

I Heard the News Today, Oh Boy

Maybe compared to someone else, your circumstances aren't so extreme.

Damnit! It's May 4 and I heard the worst news. Be warned. This is where the love story turns grim and depressing as Jakie succumbs to the cancer. If you choose to fast forward to the more uplifting and inspirational parts of my lover's tale, I understand. That would have been my preference.

We've been back home for two weeks and Jakie's not doing well. Pain, pain, pain, massive pain. Her kidney is blocked and her back hurts like hell. I don't sleep. The doctor told me Jake's lungs are filled with cancer. No big surprise; I knew it was coming, but it's really, really—sad. Damn, I keep hearing that f*ing conversation with the doc over and over.

This morning, I asked God to be with me and help me take the bad news. I can't believe that after all I've been through I can still be shocked. Do you know what it feels like, to be told that it looks bleak, her lungs are filled with a blizzard of cancerous dots, and all we can do is make her comfortable for her remaining time? That's a question I hope no one ever has to answer. When the oncologist laid it on me, with all the authority of his schooling and the totality of his training, I went south.

I heard the words; I expected the words; I already knew it, but still my stomach hit ground zero and I doubled up. I didn't sob; I wailed, I caved in. I don't want to be alone. I don't want her to leave. I feel so helpless, helpless to the helpless feeling gnawing inside me every time Jake yelps in pain—horrible ten out of a possible ten pain, constant, worse than kidney stone pain.

Without the comforting awareness I now possess—that Jakie was and is fine—I pondered what our house will be like without her. Bobby cried. His mommy's not getting better and he wants to know why they can't they get rid of the tumor. I feel so empty inside. I don't have an answer. Tonight, Jakie told me, "Mike, go get a girlfriend; find someone to talk to." I can't believe it: With all she's gone through, she's still thinking about me and wants me to be happy, she loves me so much. It's so poignant. She's going to go on a higher dose of pain medication. We're going to make her comfortable. What about the rest of us?

Happy Birthday

We are all a consciousness of Light. Simply by asking, we can bring it forward. It carries an energy that makes things better.

April 4, 1999. It's the fifty-somethingth anniversary of my birth and Dr. Rau is concerned. Who isn't? He said there's no orthodox treatment that can help Jakie. No crap, it's thirty grand later and what the hell does he think we're doing here? Happy Birthday, Mike!

I don't tell Jake what he said, and I wonder if I'm being strong, holding Dr. Rau's pessimistic words inside of me. Or am I being weak, not revealing the truth? This is virgin territory for me. Damn, I have to tell the kids when we get home.

That night as Jakie slept, I heard the following words in my mind and wrote them down.

"Michael, surrender to God. Give up your burdens. Let God have them. You can't control anything. Let everyone have their destiny. Let Jake be free. Let your kids be free. Be free. Only God decides who lives and dies and when it's time to go. You can't control it. God wants your burdens. He wants peace for you. There is so much joy in God's will. Surrender to God. You say it; now do it. Surrender to God. Let God's will be done. Stop the struggle. God wants you to be peaceful. God wants to care for you. God loves you. Give him the pain; give him the worry. Let Jake do her thing. Love her and assist her. Don't hold her back. Surrender to God. God will take care of you. Surrender." I wonder if we're here on a healing journey or a spiritual one. On the other hand, maybe they're one and the same.

The next day, more bad news. Jake's CEA, that relentless indicator, shot up to a hundred and fifty something. Another number showed pancreas involvement, which goes with kidney involvement and all the other involvements and this penetration and that penetration. Damn! I remember when penetration was a feel-good word.

I hate the medical side of all this disease stuff. I am more of an essence type guy. That probably explains why I spent most of the day crying in the bathroom, wiping my tears, before coming out and being strong for Jakie.

It was a day of despair and burden. None of the treatments are working. This place is either a fraud or she is somehow blocking what they have to offer. The chemo at home didn't work either. They gave her a new pain reliever. I can't read it—it's in German—but it works. A few drops and the pain is gone. That's good, and with Jake out of pain, we decide to go out to dinner at La Dolce Vita, the Italian restaurant in Teufen, run by a Portuguese family, where most of the Swiss clientele smoke. So with her doped up and me quaffing a fair amount of Schützengarten beer, we are resigned to Jake's imminent death. We survive through a pleasant and amusing dinner with our other diseased friends and she's still alive. What to do?

It reminds me of the first few days after Jake was diagnosed. As soon as she heard the news, she took to the bed to await the end. She went through a kind of panic and did a lot of praying. Three days later, she was still here and with all that extra rest, she was filled with vitality and spunk. So she got up. She was still here then, and she's still here now.

Back in our room, I quickly fall into a beer-induced dream. Jakie lifts me out of my body and we float upward, higher and higher through misty clouds, past flying puppies and floating footballs, until we reach a beautiful sanctuary oasis. We sit surrounded by emerald green and purple light. A bountiful buffet is set up next to the bar, where we sit mesmerized by each other's gaze. She takes my hand and with a chime transforms herself into Tinkerbell and says, "Michael."

"You are so cute."

"Michael, pay attention!"

"No, I want to make out."

"Michael!" She turns herself into a massive pillar of Light. "Listen to me!!"

"Yes, dear."

"It's time for you to know. I am going home to God."

"No," I wail. "Stay with me."

"I am about to graduate. This lifetime, my last one on earth, was devoted to completing unfinished business. My job was to lead you back to God and love a family and a stepchild. I have accomplished that; there's nothing more for me to do."

"Does that mean you're dying?"

"Yep," she informed me cheerfully.

"No!!"

"It's only a matter of time for this body to give out. Life, after all, is a terminal condition," she says, laughing and kissing me. "Sure it'll hurt," she continues, "but it can't be much worse than giving birth to a baby. Shoot, you know I can handle that."

"That makes me so glad I'm a man," I inexplicably blurt.

"The joy of holding a newborn creation is as pleasurable and blissful as it gets on earth. And now it's time for me to move on to the joy of my new life. Being held by God. Finally. Fully. Completely. It's too tempting an offer to pass on."

"But, you're hurting so much; don't you want to keep fighting?"

"From the second I was diagnosed, Spirit has been protecting me from the pain by lifting me into a transcendent state. It's like I've been watching it from above myself."

"How can you leave us?"

"Shit, man, we've all died so many times before, it's no big deal."

"It is to me."

"My higher self is elated at this wonderful opportunity. One foot in heaven and one foot on earth and I can lean into whichever side I want. I've had a lot of practice runs lately moving from physical to spiritual space."

"So you're kind of halfway there?"

"Yeah, back and forth."

"You're amazing," I marvel at her. From this elevated place, even I can find a little peace.

"It's not me doing it. I've found a place inside—something very profound, a sacred space. It's a place that has wisdom, is all-knowing; it's a place that we can attune to, that communes to us, speaks to us, guides us, and when we reach it, it can be so valuable and comforting."

"What is it?"

"It's been called the heart, the inner master, an inner guide, the Spirit within, the Self. Maybe it's simply a quiet space where we can go for greater wisdom. Maybe it's our soul, which is connected to God. It doesn't matter. What does matter is, something profound resides inside of us, waiting patiently for the call."

"Why can't I have that?"

"You can. You do. Everyone has it. It comes with the physical initiation, being born. Be still and breathe, Michael. Ask for it. All you have to do is ask. Listen to your Self. Listen for your inner voice. It's a part of you. It's your friend—a constant friend who doesn't lie, who has knowledge beyond the obvious. It has access to healings, serendipities, direction, and blessings. It's the comfort inside that offered you the blessing of becoming the lone tree, so you could give me a little relief. It's the sweetness that nurtures you, as you hold constant, never wavering, in your loving and caring for Jakie. It's the source of this dream."

Then, as she slowly levitates to join the floating chickens in the sky, she winks and says, "It's a good thing we're not our bodies."

When I wake up in the morning, I experience Jakie in a different light. Sure it was a dream, but that faraway, contented look in her eyes makes me wonder. Jake has gone through a change of consciousness here. She is totally peaceful and serene, ethereal and otherworldly, soft and loving, an angel flying too close to the ground.

Meanwhile, back on Planet Earth, we have a really nice weekend. We take an excursion to St. Gallen to find souvenirs to bring home for the kids. There is nothing. The only homegrown Swiss/German t-shirts are crudely pornographic, with cartoons of drunken guys with red noses and other things. All the other t-shirts are in English, except for one that reads, "Der Simpsons." We get one for Bobby since he's a big "Der Simpsons" fan.

Another choice is to get them something at one of the fancy adult clothing stores, but my kids never like what I buy them in Los Angeles and damn if I'm going to return something to Switzerland. I guess it's a round of Swiss army knives and a bag of Ricola cough drops.

Conversation Number Six

Transform yourself to loving, to truth-full-ness. Ask what is false about yourself and look at it.

Jakie's been in heaven for two months and we just got a job. I'm writing a pilot for the Disney Channel based on something Jake and I pitched last year. I was really sad when I got the deal, because I didn't have anyone to share the news with. The kids said, "Tell Jake," and I cried out, "Baby, I got a gig." I heard her reply, "I know. Who do you think got it for you, dummy?"

We're still in contact, but she's much less like Jake and much more like a voice from Spirit; "The Love of Spirit," is what she calls herself now. She's weaning me from Jakie, breaking that connection. Thank God for this spiritual knowingness. I don't know how people do this grieving thing without the assistance from a higher power. Life can be so heartbreaking.

I asked The Love of Spirit if she had anything else to tell me about what's going on in heaven. And she replied, "I was in a place, a vegetable kind of garden where they had kind of green string beans and pods—vegetarian fibers. It's like collagen. It's a heavenly version of the garden of earthly pleasures, except it's not sexual. Everything is so complete, full, and whole, there are no needs. It's fun and exciting, but it doesn't have an addictive pull. It's like glue, or a material that fills up the addictive need. The energy of this garden is being fed into you and your addictions will slowly dissipate and eventually be gone. It doesn't mean you can't drink or have sex or anything like that; just the pull, the need to do it, will be gone. We're taking the addiction out, so your obsessive needs will be gone. That's a big one for you, Michael. Just do the things you choose to do and enjoy everything. I went there for you and you have knowledge of that."

After I told her I was feeling pretty good, she gave me some advice: "You don't know it, but a lot of people look up to you. A lot of people up here look up to you. A lot of people down there look up to you, too. Keep the humility; it's good. Relax and enjoy yourself. You can't drink too much. Don't judge it. You deserve a good night's rest."

"Okay," I replied and still curious, I asked, "Did you do any work for God today?"

"Yes, I floated thru hell on a mission."

"Pardon, is that what you said?"

"Yes."

"Did they notice you?"

"No, they were too into their own stuff. They were kind of demented."

"I'm lonely, baby."

"No you're not. You just don't have a woman; that's one of your addictions. It's pleasant to spend time with a woman, exchange energy with a woman, but you don't need that. You need friends—to be with people."

"Before you went and crossed over, you told a friend there's something you had to tell her. What was it?"

"She's to get on her knees and thank the Holy Spirit for giving her this new life of sobriety and with it comes a great, deep burning desire to serve and make the world softer for others. She was blessed and she is to extend blessings. She is participating in the giving and receiving cycle and she's to know she's totally worthy of God's love, from this moment forward. The slate is wiped clean by her turning to the Light. It's as simple as her accepting it."

"I could sure use a babe massage, Jakie doll." I was trying to suck her into a little flirting, but The Love of Spirit wasn't buying. She stayed on purpose.

"Your directive is to continue to make your transition from me being there. Keep cleaning up and things of that nature while repeating, 'Here I am God; where do you want me?' Michael, I love you. I love the boys. It's quite a miracle of loving that you and I created. And remember, your goodness and your loving takes you to the heavenly level you raise to when you die."

I guess the Beatles were tapping into some higher place in *Abbey Road*, when they reminded us that the love we take with us when we die is equal to the love we make while we're here.

Boundless Love

The End of the Beginning

This is not our home. Our jobs don't go with us.

It's the morning of our flight home and I hold my frail little Jakie next to me. I am shivering in the snow, waiting for the car to pick us up and take us to the airport. Well, was it worth it? On the plus column, her attitude and inner consciousness have shifted. She's much more with the God thing. There appears to be more Spirit working with her than there has been in a long, long time. As for me, all I can think about is I've got a lot of luggage and logistics to carry on my tired shoulders.

I have two thoughts. The first is to neutrally observe everything going on from an elevated viewpoint. If someone else were in Jakie's predicament, I'd say, "God bless you, I'm delighted you're going back to God," and I would appreciate God's perfect plan. "How wonderful, an angel going to heaven, back to the great ocean of love and mercy. Bless your magical life and all the magnificent times and delightful friends. God is good."

But then there's little Mikey—me. I'm at a loss. I feel so dejected that my heart can't break anymore. I think about her small insurance policy helping out with our gargantuan debt. "Ours?" Where she's going, she's not going to be able to make monthly payments. It won't be too long before I become the sole owner of *our* debt.

Back on Sutton Street, the kids finally know what's going on and they're acting weird. I can't remember if I told them or they figured it out. I've been constantly by Jakie's side, hardly talking to them. Eli is moving around in a daze. Bobby is gloomy and Joey is anxious.

During breakfast, I heard an inner voice tell me, "If I love God through all of this, my whole family will go straight to heaven." I like that thought, because that's definitely where Jakie is going and it will be nice for us to all be together again. Then my mind continues to do its insanity. "There's good news in all this—at least Jake won't have to finish all that expensive dental work."

Bobby gets his driver's license this summer and wants the car, but Eli is older and has dibs. They argue. The mundane goes on in the midst of my first-ever, life-and-death moment. Game five of the Lakers-Kings series is coming up tonight. It's win or go home. Jake is going home to be with God. Who can fault her for wanting that? I am the Sacramento Kings, going home a loser.

I feel like a cursed Shakespearean character. Nothing ever works out. I've kept it mostly positive, as good as I could, better than I thought possible, since the day my sweetie was diagnosed. I guess positive thinking doesn't work. What else are you going to hit me with, God?

Both Bobby and Eli asked me how long their mom was going to live. What a question. I told them, "I don't know; only God knows." That's the truth and it sounds like so much bullshit. The sum total of life is bullshit.

Jake is very delicate, almost airy. She needs everything calm and quiet. She sends me out of the room if I get upset. Like every second. Do you know how hard it is to be cheerful? To look at your loved one—pale and cute and vulnerable, whose energy radiates only love—

and know she is filled with raging cancer? She's put me on a strict, positive word diet. She is very clear about what I may and may not say. I am not permitted to utter anything negative. It's really strange that two people who've spent so much time gossiping and conniving together, talking out the smallest crap and sharing the minutia of our lives, are not talking much these days. Jakie is totally internal and I have been censored. I'm not complaining, at least not out loud.

I wonder how my kids are going to take it when Jakie splits. I've spent every waking hour of my life protecting them. They've been the most loved and cared for children and they show it. Jake and I have been home almost continuously, writing a lot, but still around. We butter their bread and cut their meat. We quiz them for exams; we make Bobby a healthy lunch every day. I make sure they take their vitamins and supplements. Their lives have been idyllic; they've lacked for nothing. In spite of my pessimism, I have always been optimistic about the future. They've been emotionally hugged and loved. Life for the Weinberger kids has been a carnival, a celebration since the day they were born. Now they're twenty, eighteen, and almost sixteen. Once they were little—an energetic puppy pile. Mom and dad showed up at every soccer, baseball, and basketball game they played. We both coached. I was thrown out of a pee wee basketball game with two technical fouls. Jake coached Eli in hoops. I don't think Eli made an outside shot that year, but he still made all stars. The love we showered on our kids made them awesome. They're confident self-starters, naturally expressing their talents, in their flow; they are successful because that's who they are. And now, this test.

One of my closest friends, John Morton, sent an email today. He wrote, "Love Jake healthy or love her into God's arms." I guess that's the answer. Love, no matter what.

I am so typically typical. I have a house with no chimney. I never got it fixed after the Northridge earthquake, because we lived off the insurance money. I'm borrowing from Peter to pay Paul, the shower is leaking, and interest rates are going up, and I worry about Bobby's playing time, Joe's grades, and Eli's partying. I thank the Lord that I live a multidimensional existence, because I can go nuts on a lot of different levels at the same time.

Next fall, Eli will be back at Duke and Joe will be at USC. It'll just be Bobby and me, and I wonder if I should I sell the house and why there is a gas smell. Great, now the stove is broken. Let's just add that to my neuroses, anger, petulant outbursts, hurt feelings, failures in business, credit card bills, and broken heart. Man, life didn't prepare me for this. Michael, stop thinking! God is in control. God can heal her in a flash if He wants. I will love her healthy or love her into God's arms. I'm in support of God's will and will love Jakie, in or out of this world. I so want to believe that we continue to live on, past this existence. Jakie says that's the case, that we've lived and died lots of times before. Even before she did anything spiritual, like when she was a little girl, she said she used to think back and couldn't ever remember being dead. She remembered all the way back and knew she was always alive. She's taught me so much.

It's four in the morning and I wake up to the sound of barfing. Jake has the dry heaves. The doctors think it's from new lesions on her liver. Whoopee. The kids are seeing the reality of the situation. But really, what is reality? Maybe earth is the dream, a bad dream, and heaven is real.

The oncologist wants me to come in and talk realistically. He wants to put Jake in a hospice. Trust me, that's not going to happen. No one is taking care of her but me! I love this job. I love having her around, kissing her, feeding her. I don't care how sick she is. Every day is precious; she's not going anywhere.

"Dear God, please be with our family as we go through this difficult, difficult transition. The odds suck, but God, you could heal her instantly. Bless my wife, hear my prayer, and bless my family. Prepare us. Help me meet my expenses. Help me send my boys to school. Fill me with courage. Bless me with the strength to care for and nurture my family. I am your humble servant. Hold me in your arms, anoint me, and let me travel to your great ocean of love and mercy. Amen."

I told my mom that I believe we don't die. Sure, the body we're given to lug around this lifetime drops, but the soul moves on. I'll be reunited with my loved one soon enough. I told my kids the same thing, and although they instinctively buy it, they told me to shut up!

Happy Mother's Day. Jake is sleeping next to me, wheezing, as we listen to Andrea Bocelli's tearful rendition of "Time to Say Goodbye." Thank god most of it's in Italian, because I'm sure I couldn't handle it if I understood the words.

I sip my wine and assume Jake is a goner. She is a rail, not eating, pale, dormant, quiet, and separate from me. Codeine and Vicodin are wiping her out, making her nauseous, and then we give her a suppository to handle the vomiting, and all of it causes dizziness and hallucinations. Basically, that leaves no one home to fight the cancer.

I called the kids together for a family meeting. We took a vote and said a prayer. We didn't go, "Oh God, keep her with us." We voted, the brood and me, "Dear God, if you're not going to get her better, take her quick." Everyone was in agreement and I am glad for that. This isn't our Jakie. It's getting pretty intense. She slept all day, changing t-shirts two extra times because of lung lesion sweats. The weight is dropping off her like mad.

There has been some discussion of intervening surgically and draining her blocked kidney, the suspected cause of the pain. It's an option, the only option. If they can reduce the pain to a two or a three, it's possible that she can get off the medication and get some vitality back. She says she feels like a dope addict. Everyone involved in Jake's care thinks we have to go for it, get that surgery. We've got to get her eating. She's afraid of more medical intervention and doesn't want to be pricked and poked at anymore, but I don't see any option.

I'm not ready to let her go. Not even when she tells me, in her sweetest, most darling voice, "Michael, it's time to go to the hospital."

When we arrived, Jakie got real grumpy because they didn't have a bed ready. Damn, was I happy to be yelled at, it's been so long. I miss getting nagged. Please, baby, yell at me some more. Look, I didn't pick up my socks; see, there are wet towels all over the floor. Call me a slob; tell me to shut up.

I was utterly exhausted and I left as soon as the nurses had her comfortable. That's when another miracle occurred, in the form of Mike Sullivan. Shortly after I left, Mike, who lives close by, stopped by the hospital to see Jakie. The nurses told him she wasn't going to make it through the night. Of course they didn't tell me, but thanks to his call, I got the boys together. I could have messed up big-time, but Spirit wouldn't let me.

Our family had wonderful closure. The kids showed up at the hospital on "the fateful night," the night she was about to blast off. Jakie was tripping out; you could see in her eyes that her soul, her essence, was somewhere else. Yet when the kids held her hands and softly called, "Hi, Mom," she came back into her body and her eyes were alert. She lit up with so much love when she saw them. I am crying as I remember this. She loves her boys so much. She held their hands and showered each of them with the energy of heaven. The kids sobbed and wailed and loved her back with every ounce of their hurting little hearts.

It was perfect—probably the most powerful moment of my life. Not one of us feels any emptiness or the sting of something left unsaid. She graced each of us with our individual loving moment, showering her greatness upon us. When I said I loved her with all my heart, she waved me away with a matter-of-fact, "I know." We were complete and had been for a long time.

When we got home, the guys and I stayed up into the morning and had so many laughs and so many tears. Joey asked, "You want me to hook you up with some babes, Dad?"

"Give me like a week," I replied facetiously. There was some joy in this. We have our own little fraternity. We called Dave and he came by real late and we hugged and cried and laughed some more. I said to the gang, go live your lives, but don't leave me alone; leave one person here at least until after dinner.

When it was almost over and she was down to less than ninety pounds, we would sit in bed and I'd hold her hand and tell her I loved her. I told stupid jokes to make her smile. Tears flood my eyes as I see her in my mind. Even in the hospital, with her oxygen mask askew, she was beautiful. I was steadfast. I've been on a mission to save her. I was relentless; I never gave up. I saw her healthy to the end, as healthy as the day we met, with her red plaid flannel shirt and dancing blue eyes. I swear that's what I saw. We lived and she died in our enchanted cottage.

May 18, 2000. Jakie's graduation day.

A Collect Call from Spirit

*The world has an amazing quality and quantity of distraction.
Use it to your advantage.*

Hooking up with Jakie on the cosmic cell phone was so much fun, I tried it all the time. I remember once slipping into bed, sipping tequila, and inviting Jake to join me. "I'm here, baby," I said.

But she didn't come. I listened in the silence, waiting and waiting. No answer. I called out again. Nada. Eventually I closed my eyes, and resting my head on the pillow, I heard the following words.

"To Michael from Spirit. You were the tree. You held and you nurtured. You swayed in the vicissitudes. You bent but never broke. You were the calm and the strength, the fiber and the tears, the roots and the neutrality, the nurturer and the nurtured. You provided protection and comfort in all the shades of shade. You are a long-standing soul and you will be nurtured from the same great well of gratitude and service of which you gave. All honor to you and your family. The gates of heaven open and sing their praises unto you and yours, for the past, the present, and the future. You are the tree—strong, beautiful, quiet, calm, and neutral. All peace is yours. God loves you and is so glad to have you and Jakie back in his arms."

Whoa, the hits keep right on coming. Today, I was shopping for the kids' dinner and I ran into an old friend of Jakie's—a very sweet, warm woman from pre-school days I hadn't seen in years. "Hey Mike, how you doing? How's Jakie?"

Obviously, she hadn't heard. I thought about it for a spell and finally said, "Jake's doing quite well." Well, she is. I've got to admit it was fun for me to do that—a little irreverent, but I couldn't bear getting pulled back into someone else's shock and fear. I didn't want to get into talking about what kind of cancer killed her, how long it took, and all the grim details. It was just easier.

Spirit Rides on Love

If I'm going to be involved with you, we're going to have a good time. I insist on it.

I've been considering everything Jake told me about dying and I'm trying to relate it to her experience, both when she was here and after she moved on. She was amazing. I watched her move from her human part to a more spiritual side during her transitional time. At some point, she stepped into that transcendent energy and accepted her fate.

Certainly, by the time we got home from Switzerland, she wasn't struggling anymore. But it's strange—she was still interested in *Hardball* with Chris Matthews and talking about painting the bedroom. It confused me, probably herself, too.

In spite of being that young and having all those pulls to stay here, somewhere along the way, she surrendered and wanted to be with God. I also imagine that at some point Spirit comes in and lifts us and loves us and shows us how.

What she taught me going through her process is there's very little apprehension about dying. Coming into the far turn and roaring down the stretch, Jakie was pure and childlike. I called her *Jakadette*, my takeoff on the old movie *The Song of Bernadette*, which she loved. Like Sister Bernadette, Jake had nary a complaint as she approached her death—only the slightest little fear. Most of us die with our grudges, our hates, our resentments, and our annoyances. Not Jakadette.

I am doing my best to follow Jake's directive to be happy, but when people call or I think of something from the past, I break down. When I wake up in the morning, the bedroom is really weird. I sleep so tightly on my side of the bed, so I don't roll over and hurt her. When we get loving letters, I want to go, "Hey, Jake, we got a —." Oh yeah, she's not here. That's how we lived. We shared everything and filled each other up in a really positive way.

I go for long walks and cry. I wasn't prepared. Even expecting the inevitable, I was shocked by how quickly it ended, but knowing Jake, she wasn't going to spend much time being sick and in pain—that wasn't my sweetie's scene. No way. No holding on; as soon as it got tough, she said get me out of here. "I'm losing, I quit."

I judge myself so much. I completely concur with the sentiments of pioneer hip-hop legends Grandmaster Flash and the Furious Five, life can be a jungle sometimes, and many's the time I wondered how I kept from going under. I put myself down and beat myself up because I'm afraid I didn't do enough to help her. Like, two nights before her final liftoff, Jake was having big trouble breathing and I didn't do very much. I didn't realize she was in the final stages. I thought she was overmedicated. On the other hand, her exit was beautiful, just how God would orchestrate it. I didn't play God at all.

Shortly after Jakie died, I spoke to a close friend who possesses a huge heart and vast spiritual knowledge. As I expressed my feelings, tears welled up and I started to cry; and while I was in that weepy, tearful, and sorrowful state, my loving friend told me, "The Holy Spirit won't come in on that. Spirit doesn't come in on grief, or tears, or anything else negative. Spirit rides on love. Spirit is alive and dynamic. Joy is a sign that Spirit is present."

Okay! That's where I want to be. I want Spirit working in my life. I want joy and lightness, so I pulled myself together. *However*, I never held back one tear. I was hurting and when it was time to cry, I cried. It didn't matter where or when or who or why or what. I honored my pain, my loss and despair. I cried everywhere you can imagine. It felt good. It was therapeutic and sweet. I remember once bawling so loudly, sitting alone in the living room watching Prince sing, "I Would Die 4 U" in *Purple Rain*, that Bobby ran in to see if I was all right. It was one of Jakie's favorite songs. Art imitates life.

Grieving is one of life's natural occurrences. Something triggers something and tears are attached to that and I allow the tears to flow. I cry and ask people to bear with me for a minute or ten. I never know when or where the tears will burst forth. Doing business about her death, I cried when I had to write her social security number. Whatever was attached to that came pouring out.

Jakie had every attribute of an admirable woman. She had strength, she had intellect, she had humor. She had heart. She had it all. She raised those kids with total commitment, kept a career going, and was totally available to me. She was awesome. Her body took her as far as it could and now she's back doing God's work. I am very proud of her and I'm also proud of me. I never knew how strong I could be. No one did. For the past year, I was more committed in my intention of healing her than anything I ever did. But being strong for a cause, even a losing cause, was more than just a show of strength. It was integrity, commitment, and love. It was my best work ever.

When we met, we made a vow to always have fun and we kept our word. As long as she lasted, we kept putting our faith forward and did everything possible to pull down the miracle. Jakie was tough, a powerhouse, and healthy in her cancer; her core stayed strong in the midst of terrible disease. Before Switzerland, the doctors told us there was no hope whatsoever. So what, we went and tried. She still had vitality, enough vitality that you would say it could be possible.

Was Switzerland worth it? Absolutely. We made the trip a vacation, a honeymoon. It snowed; it was an elegant setting. Who's to say it wasn't perfect for us to share the time together in a beautiful place?

As the days floated by, I experienced some powerful spiritual moments. One time, I not only felt that Jake was with me, but also, on a multidimensional level, I felt so strongly that I was with her in Spirit. There was no separation. I was there and she was here; we were everywhere together. When we were young, sometimes when we made love we couldn't tell where one of us began and the other ended. That was hot. This was hotter. We are all one. I got that real deep, on an experiential level. And also, at the same time, I felt the love of my family, the love that Jake and I created, the love for each other, and the love for each kid, in every combination. It was out there, it was here, it was real and obvious, and I kind of pulled it in and put it on and it became enormous. I'm expanding like crazy. Maybe I should feel worse to honor Jake's memory, but that's a lot of bull, because I know Jake is here.

My life's been magical, even when it's been horrible. Jake's last year was pure tension, total tension. It was also the greatest year of my life—the most blessed. I loved taking care of Jakie. No one has the closeness we had. I was so fortunate.

The house is quiet. The kids are out being kids and I'm alone most of the time. I sit in front of the TV flipping channels, watching Procul Harum sing, "A Whiter Shade of Pale," on VH1 Classic, sipping wine and being bored, when I get this really weird thought and crack myself up. I miss our fights. Really, when there was nothing on TV, what better way to spend an evening than to go at it, get the adrenaline pumping.

Of course we fought; we were married. Sure, we yelled and screamed and left perfect doorknob-size holes in the drywall from slammed doors, but we had a rule. As soon as someone laughed, it was over; you had to drop it. Once you got your laugh, it was finished. We cut that deal early on and since we were both pretty funny, our battles never lasted that long. Oh, one other thing about a good fight is you always get to make up.

I start to plan the memorial service. Jakie says the service is not for her; it's for the living and I should tell everyone she's fine. I guess her ultimate message is, "It's better to be dead."

Three Years Later

What I can't deny is the love—ordinary, fundamental love. My loyalty is to uphold the loving.

About a week and a half before Christmas 2003, I took a trip to a spiritual retreat in Northern California. Gliding up Interstate 5, I made a mockery of the speed limit. It's a dull, smelly voyage, especially passing the lounging cattle of the Harris Ranch, reeking with the all-pervading pungency of cow poop. Later, cutting to the coast, I cruised through Gilroy, the garlic capital of the world, and was inundated with the zesty aroma of garlic, mixed in with the remaining wafts of bovine dung that followed the car.

Which reminds me, the spiritual gathering, called *Living in Grace*, took place at the Asilomar Conference Grounds, next to the ocean in Pacific Grove. According to their literature, "The Asilomar Conference Center is a 'refuge by the sea.' As a member of the California state park system, Asilomar offers 107 extraordinary acres of forests, dunes, and coastline. Deer graze in the forests and meadows, while woodpeckers and squirrels gather in the pines; seals bask on the rocks and otters swim in the coves; and, when the season is right, the whales breech and spout offshore and monarch butterflies fill the air." I love Northern California. Beautiful trees, crisp clean air. It's a whole different world.

Asilomar is ten minutes away from Carmel and since my girl-friend—aka, primary relationship? main squeeze? significant other? partner? (what are people our age supposed to call each other?)—and I arrived for the divine festivities a day early, we decided to lunch in the touristy township. Huh, whatdidyoujustsay? Girlfriend? Relationship? Hold on, hold on, more about Marya later.

Carmel is a fun place for people with too much money. Their colorful propaganda proclaims, "There are few places on earth as incredibly dynamic, yet so quaint and picturesque. Nestled in a pine forest above the spectacular white-sand beach, the one-square-mile village offers endless vacation and cultural opportunities. Stroll the charming streets and explore the village's numerous unique shops and fine restaurants and relax in one of our outstanding B & B's, Inns or Historic Hotels. You'll have a wonderful time no matter what you choose to do in Carmel-By-The-Sea."

I chose to check out the conspicuous quaintness and as we explored the art and photo galleries, the tchotchke shops, and clothing stores for farto white people, I felt myself invisibly pulled into the China Art Center—an eclectic shop that sells antiques, paintings, screens, embroidery, and jewelry. That's where I met the extraordinary Sister Asha.

Asha is an oval-shaped Chinese American woman with short, black hair, twinkly eyes, and a quick wit. She was raised by a Jewish doctor in Hollywood and now sells Chinese art and knowledge. Besides English, she speaks fluent Chinese, which she flavors with words like *oy*, *meshpucha*, and *chutzpah*. She's also startlingly psychic.

As I was buying Mike Sullivan's Christmas gift, the beautiful Chinese calligraphy symbols of *Love* and *Blessings*, Sister began to read my beads. She probed into my bond with Marya and asked about my relationship with Jakie. She advised me—without my asking, mind you—that this was a good time to give Jake back to God. Huh? I was kind of surprised, because I thought I had pretty much completed that over the past three years. But I was open and decided to take a look at the prospect of a deeper release.

During the following days of meditation, spiritual exercises, and group sharing, I reflected on Asha's words and my relationship with Jakie, especially since she died. No doubt, I had applied a great deal of love and healing to my hurt and grief, but as I probed, I realized there was still more embedded in there. That's when I set a personal intention to free myself completely.

To my amazement, I began shedding huge pools of subterranean cleansing tears, interspersed with howls of healing laughter. It was a wild ride with enormous emotional swings. One miraculous moment stands apart. Sitting opposite my friend Agapi, I felt Jakie swoop in from Spirit and cover me, inside and out. It was surreal, fantastic. Jakie's essence, her heart, her sensuality, and her love enveloped me. It was divine. Paradise. Blissed out, I was suspended on vapors. It *was* Jakie, human Jakie, just as I remembered her. I surrendered, savoring the experience. I floated into her energy—safe, secure, loved. It was overwhelmingly comforting, astonishingly real, and heart-wrenchingly sad, as first-class a hug as ever existed. It was also "time to say goodbye."

By the time the final morning arrived, the two hundred or so crazies—uh, I mean participants—had created a very sacred space through a group focus of kindness, consideration, and joy. Falling on my knees, I spoke directly to God.

"Dear God, I know you know I love Jake with all my heart. But mine's only a teeny weenie little human heart compared to yours. That's why I'm giving my beloved back to you and your great heart, the heart of all hearts."

The floodgates opened. What began as a whimper and a snuffle turned into deep gut-wrenching sobs and moans. Tears streamed down my cheeks, my legs wobbled, and my body started to heave with locked-in grief. I couldn't stand. I staggered to an opportune wall and continued to wail from the deepest, hurtingest, sweetest little abandoned place I could imagine. Finally, I dragged my weary body to my seat and finished my conversation with God.

"I know you love her with your great, loving, and mighty heart. I've struggled enough; I know you don't want greater hurt. She's yours now. I release her and I forgive you and I forgive Jake and I forgive all souls, as I live the rest of my life in grace. I love you and I know you know what you're doing. Amen."

January 2004

God is the kind of guy who likes surprises. The good kind.

The Christmas tree's dried out and hangovers are a thing of the past. Mostly. I'm seated at the computer, back to the work of sharing my life experience and the wisdom from Spirit, when I hear an inner voice. "Look to the past to see where your future is pulling you and understand, Jake not only loved you, she also offered her life as a vehicle for your growth and awareness." Whoa, talk about love straight from the Source.

As I stared at the blank page, I mulled over all that's happened since Jake departed. At first, I thought she rejected me, but in reality, I rejected myself. Then she taught me to love the rejected place inside. I began to realize that something very rich and precious occurred by her leaving. And then reappearing. I learned I'm not here to change the world. I only have to get along with it.

I met most of my challenges by attempting to follow Jake's message. It's pretty amazing that I was given a direct knowing of her process. It wasn't mental; it wasn't a philosophy. I had an experience.

I honestly believe there is perfection in everything going on. It was like seeing heaven in the midst of all the ordinary things.

I received the unique privilege of talking to Jake and having direct communication with her after she died. I heard her message loud and clear, and it's living inside me. I experienced the continuity of life through her. I know that dying is easy, as easy as blinking the eye and never blinking again. However, the process of dying can be incredibly tough. I understand that it's a very solemn, rare occasion when that moment arrives and we'll never see our loved ones again.

I've learned so much. Today, I treat myself much more like I treated her. I am my own fragile lover. I handle myself and everyone around me much more delicately and gently. It's like she said, I'm moving to higher love and becoming more complete with myself. But wait, I am getting ahead of the story.

Shortly after the memorial service, the frenetic fuss aimed at our family dwindled away. As our friends returned to their personal concerns, I was left with the pangs of solitude. I was miserable, broken-down, and exhausted, pissed at God and pissed at life. Defeated, I was certain I'd never catch a break. I identified myself by the challenges of my childhood. I was the scapegoat—the perceived family problem, criticized and rejected. I defined myself by the way my father treated me. I was the boy with little self-esteem and it was Jake who made me whole. Now, without her I'd be nothing. She gave me a sense of my value and beauty; she saw my strength and talent. She fought for me. She taught me to be human and kind, and now—like the title of the Zombies' oldie but goodie—she's not there. Ahh, the soundtrack of our lives.

I was livid and fuming. I've been through so much: the diagnosis; the ups and downs of a lengthy, painful death process; being abandoned, broke, and loaded down with responsibility. That bitch!! How could she do this to me? I thought she cared. My first response was to escape through a martini glass darkly.

When the Bee Gees warbled *How Can You Mend a Broken Heart*, they raised several profound questions about living with sorrow. The brothers Gibb wailed that mending a broken heart was as difficult as stopping the rain from falling or keeping the sun from shining. Pretty bleak stuff, but ultimately (possibly to make the record a hit), they asked for help to begin loving again.

I asked myself the same question—how do you mend a broken heart? It seemed impossible. Jakie and I were totally bonded. She was the only woman I truly loved. How was I going to survive? I was consumed with pain, despair, and judgment. We were the closest couple in the world. She was my twin, my soul mate. Friends looked at me with sad eyes and figured I would just bend over and die. "He'll soldier on, but he'll never make it; he's too weak. Mike's going to be crippled; he's going to collapse; he's too dependent on her. C'mon, they chewed each other's food and finished each other's sentences. Poor Mike."

But I fooled them. I fooled me, too. I've gone from a place where I thought I couldn't survive to a having a fun, albeit imperfect, loving, Spirit-filled life. I've learned stuff I wish I never had to know. I learned how to get to the other side of pain and grief. I converted it. I came through. I learned how strong I truly am—and believe me, it's amazing how strong you can be when you don't have a choice. I am an unwilling expert.

I look back and marvel at myself. Starting out in deep, dark sorrow, I've come so far. Sure, intellectually I understand that the Holy Spirit doesn't come in on grief or anger or bellyaching. I believe that Spirit rides on love and joy, that Spirit is alive, dynamic, blissful, and filled with delight. Spirit is in the moment, like Jakie's description of a heaven replete with shooting stars and fireworks. That's where I wanted to live. But I wasn't sure how to get there. I needed a concrete way to stop feeling totally shitty.

I found my way by taking Jakie's message to heart. She demanded I keep living and taking my life to the joy. I started focusing on that, and over time, I realized when I started getting depressed, as soon as I was aware of it, I could change my focal point. I could simply observe something else, like happiness, gratitude, and fun. Think about it. Did you ever notice that the guy on a tightrope never looks down? Why would he? The body goes where the eyes are looking; you look down and you fall. It's the same with depression. This was miracle information to me.

Happiness is a *choice*. Yes, a choice. I realized I could go through life and the inevitable things that happen, either laughing or crying. Life doesn't care which one I choose. It's been said, "If you want to go through hell, you cry; if you want to go through heaven, you laugh."

The reality was that I was no longer a couple or a team. It's me alone and I had a decision to make. I declared it was a time for expansion and recharging. I told myself, "I want fireworks and I want them now. Jake's going to be an angel up there and I'll be one down here. We're in different places. That's done; there is nothing I can do about it. All I can control is my attitude." I chose to have fun and be happy. I chose to live from my higher self, but do you know what's really a bitch? There were people—friends actually—who didn't like me making that choice. I discovered there are a myriad of beliefs and rules about how you're supposed to act when someone close to you dies or something terrible happens. They expect you to dress in black and feel bad, really bad, and even worse.

But my days as a people pleaser were over. Life's too damn short. I got that one from experience. Besides, I am the author of my life and I will write it as a love story rather than a tragedy. Act 1 was completed the day the Jakie years began. Jake's departure from our wonderful, uplifting, fun-coming-alive, creating-a-family dream together was the end of Act 2. Now, the Mikey years begin—the final act, the fun years of success, wisdom, and completion. This is my fulfillment time and my story will be a comedy; no one will rewrite me. My life's going to be a celebration. I'm moving forward with a great attitude, planning an awesome graduation party for myself. I will not hold back just because my heart has been broken. Now, I get to love her and love me and I'm free to love others!!!

I choose to laugh, to play, and to make an adventure out of every day. I am entitled to be happy. It's in the Declaration of Independence, for godsakes. Thomas Jefferson wrote, "All men are endowed by their Creator with certain inalienable rights, that among these are Life, Liberty and the *Pursuit of Happiness.*" And the rest of our founding fathers signed off on it.

And if I'm deluding myself, who cares? I'd rather be happy, moving forward, having a blast, smiling, and laughing.

Come on, God, let's get this thing moving.

My Favorite Beatle

Have compassion for yourself, as you would for the children you love and adore. Past any behavior.

Life can be simple, but it sure ain't easy. In the early stages of what I perceived to be my stinky new life, I spent months sadly staring into the smog on the deck of my new house.

The new house. That's a yarn in itself. Even before I put the Sutton Street house on the market, I took drastic action. I took the pictures of Jakie down and put them in storage. Was I being cold? Maybe, but I call it ruthless. Every time I gazed upon the photos of my beautiful and healthy wife playing with her brood, I'd fall apart. Putting them away was a form of self-preservation.

After that, I spent most of my time packing and potchkying around the house. That's how I came upon a wrinkled-up old piece of paper, jammed in the back of a drawer. I was going to toss it, but something said, "Open me." When I realized what it was, I held it close to my heart. It was the blessing Jake received from Spirit to help bring her loving ministry forward into the world. It still expresses who she is today.

November 17, 1984

There is a boundless love that flows in your heart and it flows like a wave that knows its way to the shore, for this love has a great movement inside, for this love equals your commitment to yourself, to the Spirit of your heart, to the God of your beingness. The love of your heart is ever sustaining. It purifies. It transcends all things. This love is powerful, is healing, it is all-wise in its audience. Therefore, seek the inner counsel, seek the counsel of Spirit, for you are of Spirit and let your ministry always guide you one-step further than your previous experience. Where there is a limit, step through it and just beyond that limit is God's grace, Spirit in all its unending formless nature. Find the ways to do this in the most practical elements of life, for God resides there. Bring this boundless love forward in your family, bring it forward in your environment and let it reach out into your world. Give of it without reason and it will reside in your heart. There is great love around you that speaks to you in many voices. Give of your love, and know that you are blessed.

When we finally moved, I needed everything new, because I was leaving the past behind. David and Lynn Raynr helped me throw a garage sale, and we sold almost everything I owned. I made a little over three hundred bucks. For my whole entire freaking life!!

Then, doggedly hitting the Sunday open houses, I found Barry, a realtor who allowed me to patiently look for the home I loved. When I found it, of course I couldn't afford it, so I bought it. It's a cool place, up in the hills with gardens and a great view. I wanted to create a place for the kids to be happy. It was a way for me to love them, plus, it gave them something to look forward to by moving. They finally had their own rooms, a place they could be proud to bring their friends. One day, I walked into the family room and found Joey playing video games with 50 Cent, the best-selling rapper, who's been shot many times. This was before 50 was signed and became a big star. Unfortunately, he wasn't signed to Capitol, Joe's label, but that's a whole other story. Incidentally, 50 was extremely polite, offering his hand with a respectful, "Pleased to meet you, Mr. Weinberger."

The new place has been amazing, yet there's a kind of sadness in it, too. Jake always wanted a nicer home than our ramshackle shack and I was never able to give it to her. Our love cottage was getting pretty rundown, and some part of me felt crummy because I was living so well. That type of thought could've stopped me cold, but I wouldn't let it. I focused on what I was doing for the kids.

Marya, the therapist, says a house is a symbol of the self, and the environment I am creating is reflective of how I am treating my inner self. My intention is to create a loving sanctuary for all of us. We deserve it. Marya? Who is this person? Hold on. Hold on.

As the school year came to a close and the new one began, I was mostly motionless and loneliness prevailed. I was stagnant, burnt out, fried. A constant stream of thoughts plagued me. I judged whether I drank too much or too little. Was wine better for me than beer? Is vodka healthier than scotch? Is it okay to check out women's breasts? How many years ago did we meet? Was it on a Monday or a Tuesday? I don't know. Jakie's the one who remembers that kind of stuff, like where we went for the kids' first haircut, what happened at birthday parties, what she made for lunch on the first day of school. I have trouble remembering what day it is.

I moped around, ole hangdog Mike. For the first time in my life, I was experiencing the oddness of not having a life plan, a blueprint. I always saw us getting old gracefully, playing with our grandchildren, and sitting on the porch together, listening to opera. And I don't particularly care for opera.

I barely talked, but invisibly inside myself during that seemingly gloomy and sedentary time, I was constantly affirming that I wanted to go about my life like it mattered—to get my pep and vitality back and have a freedom blastoff. I wanted to have fun. Oh God, did I want to feel better! I distilled my desire of what I wanted more than anything in the world down to the following words: *I am trusting God and having fun.* I began saying that sentence over and over. Over and over. Awake and in my dreams. Again and again. It was my own personal, uplifting "double your flavor, double your fun" commercial. I was hell-bent on reprogramming myself.

I also worked my butt off to stay connected to the spiritual teachings that I spent all these years pretending to understand. I knew the way out is in. Alone on the deck, I would still myself by focusing on my breath and try to connect to that inspiring quiet space inside. And a message came forward; the memo from within was quite simple: "My beloved, focus on what you want more of, the things that make you feel good." Oh, thank you, great almighty voice. Easier said than done. I speak from the ache of experience when I state that nothing tests a spiritual focus like death. At the end of their lives, many good people become extremely angry with God and feel like they are being punished. I don't blame them. Death truly tests your mettle. It tested mine big-time. And I wasn't the one who died.

I wasn't anywhere near perfect in my mental focus. In spite of my desire to keep it positive, I spent hours and hours looking backward, reliving every moment of Jake's final year. It usually made me gloomy, but surprisingly, sometimes thinking about how Jake approached her demise encouraged me. She never got depressed or reactive. She must have known she was moving on to a more glorious place. She understood she was dying into the Love. There wasn't an ounce of "why me, poor me, life's so unfair." She didn't use her dying process to blame herself or anybody else. With her as a role model, not to mention her uplifting words ringing in my ears, it was the least I could do to give being spiritually mature a shot.

Sometimes it worked and I was lifted above my feelings and inner hurts. However, there were many times when my attempts tanked, but who's perfect? I'm only a teeny weenie human, remember? Sure, plenty of times I wallowed and milked my sob story, and I discovered something really interesting doing that. I learned that emotions aren't in time. When I relived the atrocious events, I would feel just as depressed now as I did the second they were happening. Amazing. What an awareness!

There was one constant to my hanging out in the pits: I would eventually figure out that I was there. Maybe the clue was tripping on the wine corks piling up on the floor, or that I didn't get out of bed, eat, shower, or shave for weeks. Little things like that.

Hey, my heart was broken, but I never quit. I learned if I could catch what was going on inside of me, I could change it. Time after time, following Cyndi Lauper's lead, as soon as I was aware of how crappy I felt, I summoned up the will and the courage for another valiant attempt at making myself happy. That was my grand intention, my goal. That was the direction I was always moving. Who cared if I took a side trip or two or ten thousand into purgatory?

I received encouragement in the strangest ways. Paul McCartney was quite helpful. On one of my quiet days on the veranda, I read that Paul was dating again. This was astonishing news since Paul and Linda had the same kind of inseparable relationship Jake and I did, only with millions more dollars and a lot more talent. So what! Paul and I were connected in the most human of ways; we both lost the dearest love of our lives. I mean, this is a guy who supposedly cried every day for a year after Linda died. If he could find someone, so could I. Thank you, Paul. Because of you, I gave myself permission to start having more boy-girl fun. You are now my favorite Beatle.

Yes, I started dating a wonderful woman. Now, now, don't judge. Jakie encouraged me. No, actually she insisted. Look, I know this is a ticklish subject. Our culture likes us to hold onto the past, to memorialize and memorize our sorrow to prove the depth of our love. It made me sad that popular opinion wanted me to look unhappy, shrivel up, and die. When I told one friend over dinner that I was doing pretty well, he made me promise not to tell his wife, because she'd hate that I was happy. To her, if I could be happy, it meant he could be happy if she died and that would mean he didn't love her enough. I don't see this couple anymore.

Well-meaning folk wanted me to deny myself life and life's pleasures, but I didn't want to suffer anymore. Man, I've endured enough for ten lifetimes. I knew what I needed and it wasn't to be totally alone. I needed someone to talk to. Jake trained me like that.

I met Marya, the most elegant embodiment of the female form I've known, at Leslie Boyer's annual Fourth of July bash, just about the time Jake informed me someone was going to show up. We connected in a flash. A pitcher of margaritas didn't hurt, and we ended up making out on top of the coats stored in Ana Maria's bedroom. Marya is a lovely, fun, attractive, caring woman, with a secret childish side. That was definitely not what I was looking for, especially after all those years of monogamy. I was in the market for a ditsy, beautiful twenty-two-year-old with immense proportions, who had issues with her father and needed to have constant sex with someone my age to get even with him. Instead I found a woman, born of my generation, I could talk to. We spent hours on the phone. It didn't hurt that she is a psychotherapist, trained in active listening. My friend Fred Gillman was right. He predicted this.

Meeting someone new was exciting and odd. Marya thought I was eccentric. Imagine that. Is it really peculiar to have an MSG attack at the Apple Pan Hamburger counter and get all spaced out and woozy? Is it odd to reach for *nux vomica* homeopathic pellets, which work as an antidote for MSG? Is it odd that I don't eat birds—chicken or turkey? I never knew I was a screwball, because Jake and I were married so long, we were used to each other's eccentricities.

At first, even I had qualms if I was doing the right thing by dating so quickly. So I turned to the Spirit voice inside of me for guidance, the voice that knows what's good for me and what's bad, what's right and what's wrong. I quieted myself and listened and it said, "Marya." I ran that by Jake in one of our conversations from beyond and she concurred, giving me her full support and adding that Marya was like "beautiful crystal."

As I look back, I'm glad I went for it. Finding my first new woman in over twenty years didn't mean I loved Jakie any less. It wasn't like I was denying my love for her and I wasn't in mourning. What it meant was, I loved myself as much as I loved Jake and that's pretty huge. It showed how large my heart is. I found the type of person who let me articulate about Jake and everything I was going through. It wasn't, "You have to be with me now and forget about her." It's a grander concept of love.

Also, in terms of me taking comfort in the female form, there was another facet to consider—the spiritual aspect. Face it, when a person really loves you, they truly want you to be happy. From her new higher home, Jake wasn't trying to attach herself to me. She was living higher love. She wanted me to be as free as she was. It wasn't like the movie *Ghost Story* where the ghost hung around. But there's one thing I'm certain of: If Jakie were still here, she'd scratch Marya's eyes out.

Hoops

We're here to love one another and have a good time.

As the months after Jakie filled out her change of address form rolled along, an uplifting momentum gradually began to take root inside me. It happened naturally, growing out of my transformation into a single mom. My new job. I became totally focused on loving and comforting my kids and making a happy home. And, miracle of miracles, by getting totally involved in my maternal skills, I became less involved with my own pain. It was a brilliant move and makes so much sense. By loving my litter unconditionally, I received the sweetest healing for myself.

I work my butt off for my kids. I get up with Bobby, make him a protein shake, and cut his waffles. I make their doctor and dentist appointments. I pick up Joe's dry cleaning. Still do. I shop for dinner, even though I still haven't figured out how to buy for more than one meal at a time. I help with homework. I pick up towels. I am a magnificent mother. I cover my kittens' asses. "What, lost your mittens, you naughty kittens, then you shall have no pie. You shall have no pie!"

After I get Bobby off to school, like many a housewife with too much time on "her" hands, I relax with a cup of java and plan my day. Hey, moms need distractions, too. Yeah, like basketball.

"Basketball," as Dennis Hopper's character, Shooter, says in the movie *Hoosiers*, "is the greatest game ever invented." I agree. The only thing that makes it better is watching my kids play. Bobby was a varsity basketball player at Harvard-Westlake School. Thank you, God. Watching him was more than a distraction. It was an obsession, the grand obsession. It kept my mind busy, away from the pain of my loss and feeling sorry for myself. For a time, going to his games was the only thing I looked forward to. Home and away, I never missed one. I thought about games. I worried about the team, I worried about Bobby's playing time, and I worried about the coach's strategy. I suffered from hoop madness, backboard fever. I was a buckets basket case. It was wonderful.

Right after his mom died, Bobby wanted to quit playing ball. He couldn't imagine being on the court and not having Jakie up in the stands rooting for him and screaming at the refs. He stunk it up. I obsessed about that. Then, when he started going for it again, I fixated on new things: Would he be recognized for his play? Would he get more playing time? It was so much fun. The ups and downs of being a basketball parent are fantastic. The season was enthralling—even on the court.

My social life revolved around hoops and the other loving and supportive basketball families, but when I showed up with Marya at a tournament in Las Vegas, some of the wives had to adjust. Either they secretly wanted me to feel bad, or they were just plain curious.

Bobby's junior season was even better. Number 20 stepped up and became a starter. Then I had to deal with the other parents' jealousies and my own crazy thoughts. Why did he pass up that shot? Was he college basketball material? Bobby was incredible; he had overcome his low moments and was enthusiastically enjoying his success. I was there for him every step of the way as he and the team won the CIF Championship. It was big stuff. The championship game was held in front of six thousand people in the gym of Loyola Marymount University, and Bobby was in the zone. It was a blast.

In his senior year, Bobby was made captain and they lost the state championship in Sacramento to a local team with hometown officials. The only saving grace was that the game was played at the Arco Arena, where the Lakers always kick the Kings' ass.

Another wonderful diversion I leaned into for a time was the great American pastime of boozing. Boy, did I learn the art of drinking. I am certain I'm not the first person to appreciate the medicinal quality of an alcoholic beverage and the numerous educational opportunities it affords. My grandest epiphany relating to the cocktail realm concerned judgments. What I learned was that even if I drank a lot, when I made it okay, I felt okay. But, when I drank the same amount, if I went, "Oh my god, I am a piece of junk, I drank too much, I shouldn't be drinking, I'm weak, I'm not strong enough to get by without booze," I felt horrible and the hangovers were worse.

The weight of one judgment—me slamming myself, putting myself down—was worse than all the booze I drank. And then I noticed, whatever I judged was made more difficult because of my own self-verdict. So I began to cut myself some slack. I started forgiving myself, not for what I did, but for the judgment. I made it an intention to accept and enjoy everything. Even when I overdid it, I was gentle on myself. I made it okay. And I took that attitude to a ton of other fun things, like indulging in pizza, ice cream, and hamburgers.

Basically, I don't drink much anymore. Sure, I'll have a beer with you, but I am stronger now. Drinking as a way to relax and play was really fun, at a time when I really needed to relax and have some fun.

As the months turned into years, I honored Jake's directive to enjoy myself and was willing to distract myself from my pain to get there. Bobby knows the truth of this. He says, "Yeah, stuff has a way of working itself out when you're not paying attention."

January 2005

If you give God 100 percent, God will make up the difference.

I'm looking out over the Valley, down Ventura Boulevard, past the Cadillac and Saab dealerships, watching the planes taking off from the Bob Hope Airport in Burbank. I plop myself down in the teak chair closest to the hammock and allow the warm California sun to nurture my body. Life is good. My kids are in a great place. They've come thorough their ordeal beautifully and are living their lives with gusto. Eli graduated and he's back home, working as a production assistant on the sitcom *Joey*. My Joey left Capitol Records and has his own label deal at Interscope Records. At twenty-two, he's running his own company. In spite of my protests, he dropped out of school to pursue his dream. He's my mini-mogul, written up in magazines and planning major deals. Bobby's in his second year at USC, is in a frat, has been checking out the coeds, and was playing lots of pickup ball until he blew out his knee last year. Dave is a successful mortgage loan broker and just bought a condo. My heavens, the kids are getting old. Hmmm, that must mean I'm getting well into my forties.

I've learned and grown so much during the past five years. Yet the fact that someone had to die for me to mature seems like an odd kind of trade. Sure, I can be just as limitless here as she is there, but the price of that is Jakie dying. We're both at the next level. She's in a place that extends loving and grace to all, where everyone's healthy, happy, and fulfilled, and treating each other well—a gathering of loving souls. But why couldn't we be here together? Or there? It's a loss, such a great loss and such a huge gain. She did this for me. She hunted me down, chased me through many lifetimes, made me love her, and helped bring me back to God. She died so I could complete myself.

As I look back, I realize I turned a catastrophe into something very rich, and that is a gift—a very bizarre and out-of-the-ordinary gift. Today, my life is a God-given adventure. I am a joyful writer with a blessed life. My life is blessed in spite of the fact that my lover left me. It's blessed because I know, without a doubt, that she is alive in heaven. I am blessed because she's helping me from above. I am blessed because I have wonderful relationships with my friends and family. My life is blessed because of all the fun and freaky time I spent with Jakie, as she went about her work of improving and enhancing my life and the lives of our children. My life is blessed because I'm still in love with her. And Marya. Now I have two girlfriends. How many guys can say that? My heart is filled to overflowing with Jake's loving, her influence, and her sweetness. My life is blessed because I get to see her face in Eli's. I am a lucky man and she's a lucky girl. She is in a better place, a place where all the seasons are summer, having bundles and oodles of fun. It must be really cool zipping through walls and stuff; that is, if they have walls up there.

So much has been added on to me. I've overcome a long-standing beef I had with God. I have placed my life in His hands and I've experienced God's loving in an expansive way. I know it was totally out of his love that all of this took place, and Jakie would still be here if it wasn't meant to be. It's what we all needed for our next steps.

I've given up trying to control things. I'm kinder, more compassionate, and more caring. I've developed into a full-fledged spiritual being. I never conceived that I could be as complete, as full and as rich a person. I also realized how deeply I loved Jake. It's too bad that when we're living an ordinary daily life, we don't take the time to stop and cherish the preciousness of our time together. We're always busy with this and that, raising a family and working.

I've grown in my self-love and the recognition of my own soul and beauty. In some ways I idealized Jake and saw myself as the lesser; she was my angel who saved me from my darkness. Now I recognize my divinity. When she died, I was forced to look in the mirror. Even the way I talk about myself has changed: I'm much more self-honoring. I used to talk about myself as an unhappy person whom Jake completed. Losing my life partner forced me to be whole within myself. I could no longer just be the disinterested dad, now I had to be *Dad*— *Mom* and *Dad*.

I went from thinking how wonderful it was that God was with her while she was dying, to realizing how much God was also with me. I understand from my current viewpoint that I was never alone. God was always holding me, carrying me, and lifting me, even if I wasn't aware of it because I was so focused on loving Jakie. I was constantly being supported, through my dreams, her words, the inner wisdom, and even my perception of her. She's been a constant and radiant inspiration. Spirit communicated to me through her entire experience, not simply by the direct message of her speaking. It was also through her dying process, her struggle, her tears, her transcendence, her Light and Joy, and her joking around. That's not the way you usually think of someone dying. She showed me how to go through it.

Spirit was working with me, too, making my life easier. I know I'm loved, not just by Jake, but by God. That's definitely a greater message. In the midst of all our suffering and sadness, we are being constantly caressed, and when we go inside and listen, we hear the inner communication, "I'm here, beloved; I've been here all along."

I experience my partner's transition as a natural process. It's definitely not this romantic thing from the other side—all candlelight and wine and lovemaking. No, it's not, "Honey, I'm waiting for you. I'm over there and soon we'll have a little house together, a career. A puppy." Nope, it's, "We'll meet soul to soul. We had the romance; that's done." That's why she kept using lofty words like bells, vibrations, and colors, not three-bedroom homes, pools, and hardwood floors.

Certainly, after she moved on, Jake had respect for our humanness, because that's the level we're on, but she was also speaking from a higher level, a level where there's not the same attachment. That's another part of the message—to let go of this form. It makes me think of all those beautiful people who vow and promise "to love through all eternity." What they're saying is, "I'll be attached to you and keep coming back and back and back." But what if the souls aren't here the same lifetimes, or what if they pledged undying eternal allegiance to more than one soul through all eternity. It could become a cosmic joke.

It's obvious that Spirit doesn't deny our humanity. It created us that way. When our time comes to meet our Maker, we all have an aspect that pleads, "Please, God, take this thing, this bitter cup I have to drink." Of course we want the suffering to be lifted, but it's part of our humanness; it's part of knowing God, because letting go of the body is a part of God. It's part of realizing that we're not the body and God still loves us, even when we suffer. It comforts me to recognize that even as life offers up its little crucifixions, Spirit makes itself available. Even in our pain, a part of us is continuously being spoken to. That's another aspect of the spiritual experience Jakie went through, and it's included in her message.

Perhaps the greatest transformation I can credit to this blessed experience is that I am no longer afraid of dying. Believe me, when you're no longer scared, there's so much more freedom. What's the point in worrying about death? One, we don't know when it's coming and, two, moving to a more glorious place is not a bad thing. Dying is just leaving. It's natural—supernatural, if you will.

I originally believed the way to heal myself was by totally loving someone else. That's true, but there's more—there's another level, there's always another level. That's an element of Jakie's message. I've come to the realization that I am truly loved by God. If this experience was a hump I had to get over in order to know God's love, I'd pay the price. Not that I'd ask for it, but in some ways, I'm grateful. How else would I have experienced that I'm a part of God? It's astounding: Little Mikey W., a part of God? Just like everyone else. Knowing this, really getting this, makes me feel so joyful and peaceful. What's next?

There you have it; that's my love story. As the title of the Doors' four disc box set (the one that includes the explicit lyrics) reminds us, No One Here Gets Out Alive. My lover's tale is about being strong in times of stress, about choosing for your Self and finding the sacred place inside that's pure glory and perfection.

My fairy tale didn't begin when Jake got sick; it began the moment I met her. She was the first person I loved completely, with every cell of my being. And my love for Jake led me to loving myself, which led to my growth into Spirit. Like many stories, this one has a surprise ending. Ultimately, it's been about my love affair with myself. It's extraordinary that I was chosen to go through this experience and share it. I'm not a teacher or a guru. I'm just an ordinary guy, a comedy writer, and a dad.

My prayer is that you come away enriched by my story—that you go easy on yourself and know in your heart you're still okay, even as you navigate through troubled waters. Sail on, sweetie pie, sail on, your time has come. I thank you for allowing me the privilege of being your bridge over troubled waters. And rest assured, my love is coming right behind.

Here's to having fun, hanging in, getting in touch with what's inside, and holding each other during tough times. Here's to treasuring what we have and knowing there's always someone watching and listening and caring. Here's to turning our gaze from the sadness and looking to the love, as we make the choice to be happy. My Jakie offers us that as a gift. And if my little love story has helped at all, don't thank me, thank my precious little angel girl—she's the one who led the way. Cheers.

Acknowledgements

I would like to acknowledge all the magnificent friends who loved me, encouraged me and wiped my nose as I blubbered through the many drafts of this book.

Super special thanks to: Judy Jones, who took my tear stained legal pads and turned them into a word document, Lony Ruhman, my secret publishing angel and unpaid coach, Jimmie Ness, my not-as-cute-as-me twin sister from a past life, Marya Foley for her wisdom and dazzling brilliance, Connie Shaw, my Publisher, for being so much damn fun to work with, my agent Bob Diforio for finding a nurturing home for *Jakie*, Mike Sullivan for loving Jake and loving me like a big brother, Dan and Lissa Guntzelman for all their fun and generous support, Estelle Day for her grace filled approach to a fun filled life, Agapi for her generosity and enthusiasm, and Heide for loving Jake so deeply.

And to my best friends and teachers, John-Roger, who is always with me and John Morton, my mystical cheerleader.

And finally, to Janet Kathleen Anderson Smith Rescher Weinberger, my Jakie, who tracked me down through the ages and taught me how to love.

About the Author

Michael Weinberger has spent most of his adult life in television, both writing and watching it. Along with his wife and writing partner, Jake, he contributed to a generation of TV's most successful family sitcoms, writing and producing the well known *Growing Pains, Just the Ten of Us, Saved by the Bell, Facts of Life, Who's the Boss, The Tortellis, 3's Company, Alice, Laverne and Shirley, Happy Days,* and many more.

He is most proud of his four sons. Since his wife's unexpected transition, he has mastered the art of being a single mom, with one exception: the ability to plan more than one meal at a time!

Weinberger received his undergraduate degree from the University of Michigan and his Masters degree in Spiritual Science from Peace Theological Seminary and College of Philosophy.

The author lives in Sherman Oaks, CA. You can find out more about him at his website: *www.amessagefromjakie.com.*

SENTIENT PUBLICATIONS, LLC publishes books on cultural creativity, experimental education, transformative spirituality, holistic health, new science, ecology, and other topics, approached from an integral viewpoint. Our authors are intensely interested in exploring the nature of life from fresh perspectives, addressing life's great questions, and fostering the full expression of the human potential. Sentient Publications' books arise from the spirit of inquiry and the richness of the inherent dialogue between writer and reader.

We are very interested in hearing from our readers. To direct suggestions or comments to us, or to be added to our mailing list, please contact:

SENTIENT PUBLICATIONS, LLC
1113 Spruce Street
Boulder, CO 80302
303-443-2188
contact@sentientpublications.com
www.sentientpublications.com